Cathedra Veritatis
On the Extension of Papal
Infallibility

Cathedra Veritatis: On the Extension of Papal Infallibility

John P. Joy, S.T.L.
Edited by Phillip Campbell

Published by

Cruachan Hill Press
1452 Lakeside Dr.
Howell, MI. 48843

Copyright © 2012 Cruachan Hill Press
www.unamsanctamcatholicam.com

ISBN: 978-1-300-43110-7

CATHEDRA VERITATIS

On the Extension of Papal Infallibility

John P. Joy, S.T.L.

This work is dedicated
with filial love and devotion to

His Holiness Pope Benedict XVI
(2005-2013)

as also to my beloved wife
Elisabeth Anne Joy

and to our beautiful children
Maria Thérèse, Thomas Joseph, & Edmund
George.

TABLE OF CONTENTS

THEOLOGICAL NOTATION

De fide divina et catholica credenda

<u>Dogma</u>: A doctrine explicitly proposed by the Church as divinely revealed and requiring the assent of divine and Catholic faith.

De fide definitive tenenda

<u>Truth of Catholic Doctrine</u>: A doctrine explicitly proposed by the Church as theologically certain and requiring the definitive assent of Catholic faith.

Religioso voluntatis et intellectus obsequio adhaerendam

<u>Authentic Catholic Doctrine</u>: A doctrine explicitly proposed by the Church as safe, probable, etc. and requiring a religious submission of will and intellect.

Sententia fidei proxima

A doctrine implicitly proposed by the Church as divinely revealed.

Sententia ad fidem pertinens

A doctrine implicitly proposed by the Church as theologically certain.

Sententia theologice certa

A doctrine in itself theologically certain on account of its connection with divine revelation, but not proposed as such by the Church.

Sententia communis

A free opinion regarding a matter of faith or morals about which theologians generally agree.

Sententia probabilis, probabilior, bene fundata, etc.

A free opinion which is probable, more probable, well founded, etc., depending upon the strength of the arguments adduced in its favor.

ABBREVIATIONS

AAS   *Acta Apostolicae Sedis commentarium officiale*. Rome: Typis Polyglottis Vaticanis, 1909–.

AS   *Acta Synodalia Sacrosancti Concilii Oecumenici Vaticani Secundi*. Rome: Typis Polyglottis Vaticanis, 1970–1999.

ASS   *Acta Sanctae Sedis in compendium opportune redacta et illustrata*. Rome: Typis Polyglottae Officinae S.C. de Propaganda Fide, 1864–1908.

BR(T)   *Bullarium Romanum: Bullarum diplomatum et privilegiorum sanctorum Romanorum Pontificum*. Taurinensis Editio. Turin; Naples: Augustae Taurinorum, 1857–1885.

CE   *Catholic Encyclopedia*. New York: Robert Appleton, 1907–1912.

D   *The Sources of Catholic Dogma*. Translated by Roy J. Deferrari from the Thirtieth Edition of Henry Denzinger's *Enchiridion Symbolorum*. Fitzwilliam, N.H.: Loreto, 2007.

DEC   *Decrees of the Ecumenical Councils*. Edited by Norman P. Tanner, S.J. London: Sheed and Ward; Washington, D.C.: Georgetown University Press, 1990.

DTC   *Dictionnaire de Théologie Catholique*. Edited by Jean-Marie Alfred Vacant and Eugène Mangenot. Paris: Libraire Letouzey et Ané, 1903–1950.

LThK^3 *Lexicon für Theologie und Kirche*. Third Edition. Edited by Walter Kasper. Freiburg im Breisgau: Herder, 1993–2001.

MBR   *Magnum Bullarium Romanum a Leone Magno usque ad S.D.N. Clementem X.* Edited by Laerzio Cherubini. Lyons: Borde and Arnaud, 1692–1697.

Msi   *Sacrorum Conciliorum Nova et Amplissima Collectio.* Edited by Giovanni Domenico Mansi, et al. Paris: Welter, 1901–1927.

PE   *The Papal Encyclicals, 1740–1981.* Edited by Claudia Carlen, I.H.M. Ypsilanti, Mich.: Pierian Press, 1990.

Unless otherwise noted, English translations of official documents emanating from the Holy See are taken from the website of the Holy See (www.vatican.va).

INTRODUCTION

Undeterred by wars and rumors of wars, the fathers of the First Vatican Council assembled in the North transept of St Peter's Basilica to vote on the proposed definition of the infallibility of the papal magisterium. All but two of the four hundred and thirty-five fathers present called out 'placet' ('it pleases') in favor of the definition.[1] "During the proceedings a thunderstorm broke over the Vatican, and amid thunder and lightning the pope promulgated the new dogma, like a Moses promulgating the law on Mount Sinai."[2] The definition reads as follows:

> "Therefore, faithfully adhering to the tradition received from the beginning of the Christian faith, to the glory of God our saviour, for the exaltation of the Catholic religion and for the salvation of the Christian people, with the approval of the sacred Council, we teach and define as a divinely revealed dogma that when the Roman Pontiff speaks ex cathedra, that is, when, in the exercise of his office as shepherd and teacher of all Christians, in virtue of his supreme apostolic authority, he defines a doctrine concerning faith or morals to be held by the whole Church, he possesses, by the divine assistance promised to him in blessed Peter, that infallibility which the divine Redeemer willed his Church to enjoy in defining doctrine concerning faith or morals.

---

1 About sixty bishops left the council prior to this final vote in order not to be associated with its approval and promulgation, not because they disputed the truth of the doctrine, but rather the prudence of defining it.

2 Joseph Kirch, "Vatican Council," in CE, 15:307. A correspondent of the *Times* witnessed the remarkable event: "The *Placets* of the fathers struggled through the storm, while the thunder pealed above and the lightning flashed in at every window, and down through the dome and every smaller cupola. "Placet!" shouted his eminence or his grace, and a loud clap of thunder followed in response, and then the lightning darted about the Baldacchino and every part of the church and Conciliar Hall, as if announcing the response. So it continued for nearly one hour and a half, during which time the roll was being called, and *a more effective scene I never witnessed*. Had all the decorators and all the getters-up of ceremonies in Rome been employed, nothing approaching to the solemn grandeur of the storm could have been prepared, and never will those who saw it and felt it forget the promulgation of the first dogma of the Church" (originally printed in the *Vatican* [5 Aug. 1870]; reproduced by Henry Edward Manning, *The True Story of the Vatican Council* [London: Henry King, 1877], 144–45).

Therefore, such definitions of the Roman Pontiff are of themselves, and not by the consent of the Church, irreformable. So then, should anyone, which God forbid, have the temerity to reject this definition of ours: let him be anathema."[3]

With this definition the question as to whether the pope is able to speak infallibly at all has been finally settled; since then, theological discussion has centered on the subsidiary questions as to how often and under what conditions he does so. There can be no disagreement that the universally promulgated solemn dogmatic definitions of the pope are infallible, the most well known examples of which are the definitions of the Immaculate Conception and the Assumption of the Blessed Virgin Mary. Beyond this, however, we are frequently warned against the phenomenon of a "creeping infallibilization"[4] which would extend the boundaries of infallibility indefinitely. Nevertheless, there remain legitimate questions that can be raised about the further extension of the infallibility of the papal magisterium.

First of all, however, some preliminary considerations are in order regarding the terminology and structure of the First Vatican Council's definition of papal infallibility. The overarching

---

[3] Vatican Council I, Session IV, First Dogmatic Constitution on the Church of Christ *Pastor Aeternus* (18 Jul. 1870), cap. 4: "Itaque nos traditioni a fidei christianae exordio perceptae fideliter inhaerendo ad Dei salvatoris nostri gloriam, religionis catholicae exaltationem et christianorum populorum salutem, sacro approbante concilio, docemus et divinitus revelatum dogma esse definimus: Romanum pontificem, cum ex cathedra loquitur, id est, cum omnium christianorum pastoris et doctoris munere fungens, pro suprema sua apostolica auctoritate doctrinam de fide vel moribus ab universa ecclesia tenendam definit, per assistentiam divinam, ipsi in beato Petro promissam, ea infallibilitate pollere, qua divinus Redemptor ecclesiam suam in definienda doctrina de fide vel moribus instructam esse voluit; ideoque eiusmodi Romani pontificis definitiones ex sese, non autem ex consensu ecclesiae irreformabiles esse. Si quis autem huic nostrae definitioni contradicere, quod Deus avertat, praesumpserit: a.s." (DEC, 816).

[4] Wolfgang Beinert, "Unfehlbarkeit," in LThK[3], 10:390: "Im Anschluß ans Konzil setzte ein Prozeß der ‚schleichenden Infallibilisierung' ein: Mit dem Anwachsen der päpstl. Lehrautorität (Enzykliken) wächst die Neigung, ihren Äußerungen definitiven Charakter zuzuerkennen." Cf. Augustin Schmied, "'Schleichende Infallibilisierung': Zur Diskussion um das kirchliche Lehramt," in *In Christus zum Leben befreit: Festschrift für Bernhard Häring*, ed. Josef Römelt and Bruno Hidber (Freiburg; Basel; Vienna: Herder, 1992), 250–72.

statement of the definition is that the pope is infallible when he speaks 'ex cathedra', that is, from the chair of Peter.[5] One possible reading of the text enumerates five distinct conditions which must be met in order for the pope to be understood as speaking infallibly. The pope speaks 'ex cathedra' (i.e. infallibly) when:

i. in the exercise of his office as shepherd and teacher of all Christians
ii. in virtue of his supreme apostolic authority
iii. he defines
iv. a doctrine concerning faith or morals
v. to be held by the whole Church.

Some authors, such as John Henry Newman in his renowned letter to the Duke of Norfolk, hold that there are essentially four conditions of an 'ex cathedra' locution.[6] However, the official explanation of the text delivered by Vincent Ferrer Gasser, Prince-Bishop of Brixen in the Austrian Tyrol, just before the final approval and promulgation of the definition, recognizes only three essential conditions:

"The infallibility of the Roman Pontiff is restricted by reason *of the subject*, that is when the Pope, constituted in the chair of Peter, the center of the Church, speaks as universal teacher and supreme judge: it is restricted by reason of the *object*, i.e., when treating of matters of faith and morals; and by reason of the *act* itself, i.e., when the Pope defines what must be believed or rejected by all the faithful."[7]

---

[5] Cf. Ludwig Ott, *Fundamentals of Catholic Dogma*, ed. James Bastible, trans. Patrick Lynch (Rockford, Ill.: Tan Books, 1974), 286: "The Pope is infallible when he speaks ex cathedra. (*De fide*)."

[6] John Henry Newman, *A Letter Addressed to His Grace the Duke of Norfolk on Occasion of Mr. Gladstone's Recent Expostulation* (London: Pickering, 1875), 115: "He speaks *ex cathedrâ*, or infallibly, when he speaks, first, as the Universal Teacher; secondly, in the name and with the authority of the Apostles; thirdly, on a point of faith or morals; fourthly, with the purpose of binding every member of the Church to accept and believe his decision."

[7] *The Gift of Infallibility: The Official Relatio on Infallibility of Bishop Vincent Gasser at Vatican Council I*, trans. James T. O'Connor (Boston: St. Paul Editions, 1986), 45–46: "Proinde reapse infallibilitas Romani pontificis restricta est ratione *subiecti*, quando papa loquitur tanquam doctor universalis iudex supremus in cathedra Petri, id est, in centro, constitutus, restricta est ratione

The three restrictions on papal infallibility as they are described here thus pertain respectively to the subject, the object, and the act of teaching.

At another point in his speech, Gasser divides the conditions in a slightly different manner. He sets forth the essential components of the definition in four parts. Firstly, the pope is the subject of infallibility. Secondly, the act of infallibility is speaking 'ex cathedra', and Gasser explains that this is an act with a necessary condition and a necessary quality. The condition of the act is that the pope speaks precisely as supreme head of the Church in relation to the universal Church; the necessary quality of the act is that it must be definitive. Thirdly, the efficacious cause of infallibility is the protection of Christ promised to Peter. And fourthly, the object of infallibility is doctrine of faith or morals.[8] In this division, we are still dealing with three basic conditions of papal infallibility, since the divine assistance is not a condition but the cause of the infallibility. Interesting to note, however, is that the *cathedra Petri* appears in the first instance as a specification of the subject of papal infallibility, whereas in this latter division Gasser separates it from the subject (described more generally as the pope *qua* pope) and joins it instead to the act of defining as a condition of that act.[9] The first division seems preferable inasmuch as the office of universal shepherd and teacher pertains directly to the subject of papal infallibility, although it is true that it is thereby also a condition of the infallible act.

Read in this light, the core of the definition thus states that the pope teaches infallibly when:

i.   [subject:] speaking as pastor and teacher
     of the universal Church
ii. [act:] he defines
iii. [object:] a doctrine of faith or morals.

---

obiecti, quando agitur de rebus fidei et morum, et ratione *actus*, quando definit quid sit credendum vel reiiciendum ab omnibus Christifidelibus" (Msi, 52:1214).

[8] Gasser, *The Gift of Infallibility*, 73–75; Msi, 52:1225.

[9] This is also how it is described by Ott, *Fundamentals of Catholic Dogma*, 287.

This threefold enumeration of the conditions of papal infallibility is confirmed by the subsequent reiteration of the doctrine at the Second Vatican Council, which reformulated the teaching as follows:

"The Roman pontiff, head of the college of bishops, by virtue of his office, enjoys this infallibility when, [subject:] as supreme shepherd and teacher of all Christ's faithful, who confirms his brethren in the faith (see Lk 22, 32), [act:] he proclaims in a definitive act [object:] a doctrine on faith or morals."[10]

The clauses from the definition of Vatican I which appeared as conditions (ii) and (v) in the first list given above can be seen, here, not to be distinct conditions at all. A definition of doctrine binding on the whole Church simply cannot be given other than by a supreme authority, and the text of Vatican II thus relocates the reference to the authority or office in virtue of which the pope is able to speak infallibly to a position before the clause which sets out the conditions of infallibility. It is in virtue of the pope's supreme apostolic authority that his teaching is infallible when the three conditions pertaining to subject, object, and act are met. Similarly, a definition of doctrine of faith or morals solemnly promulgated by the pope precisely in his capacity as supreme teacher of all Christians cannot but be binding on the whole Church.

The subject of the infallible papal magisterium in its specific formality is thus the pope speaking as supreme head of the Church (*omnium christianorum pastoris et doctoris munere fungens*); the act which is infallible is the act of defining (*definit*); the object of this act is doctrine of faith or morals (*doctrinam de fide vel moribus*); the power in virtue of which the pope performs this act is his supreme apostolic authority (*pro suprema sua apostolica auctoritate*), which he possesses as the successor of St Peter; the result of his act is an obligation binding the whole

---

[10] Vatican Council II, Session V, Dogmatic Constitution on the Church *Lumen gentium* (21 Nov. 1964), § 25: "Qua quidem infallibilitate Romanus pontifex, collegii episcoporum caput, vi muneris sui gaudet, quando, ut supremus omnium christifidelium pastor et doctor, qui fratres suos in fide confirmat (cf. Lc 22, 32), doctrinam de fide vel moribus definitivo actu proclamat" (DEC, 869).

Church to assent to the truth of the definition (*ab universa ecclesia tenendam*); the cause of the infallibility of his act is the assistance of the Holy Spirit (*per assistentiam divinam*), who prevents him from defining erroneously; the doctrines infallibly defined are correspondingly irreformable (*irreformabiles esse*) – and against the fourth article of the declaration of the Gallican clergy of 1682, it is specified that their irreformability does not depend upon the consent of the Church (*ex sese, non autem ex consensu ecclesiae*).[11]

Outline of the Magisterium

Since this work is an inquiry into the extension of the infallibility of the papal magisterium, let us begin by situating the papal magisterium within the broader context of the Church's mission. Briefly stated, the magisterium is the Church's teaching power or her office of teaching (*munus docendi*), which pertains to faith and morals.[12] This is distinguished from the Church's office of ruling (*munus regendi*), which is related to the discipline and government of the Church, and from her office of sanctifying (*munus sanctificandi*), which refers principally to her liturgical worship and the administration of the sacraments. The magisterium is said to be 'authentic', that is, authoritative, because those who

---

[11] Declaration of the Gallican Clergy (1682), art. 4: "In questions of faith also, the duties of the Supreme Pontiff are principal ones, and his decrees pertain to all and individual churches, and yet this judgment is not unalterable unless the consent of the Church has been added to it" (D 1325). All four of the Gallican articles were declared null and void by Pope Alexander VIII, Constitution *Inter multiplices* (4 Aug. 1690). For an ample discussion of the views of leading Gallican authors prior to Vatican I, see Richard F. Costigan, S.J., *The Consensus of the Church and Papal Infallibility: A Study in the Background of Vatican I* (Washington, D.C.: Catholic University of America Press, 2005). Although presented as an historical study, one finds it difficult to avoid the impression that the author would like to rehabilitate Gallicanism under the banner of episcopal collegiality.

[12] Derived from the Latin 'magister' ('teacher'), the word 'magisterium' (although not the concept) was introduced into official ecclesiastical parlance by Pope Gregory XVI, Encyclical Letter on Church and State to the Clergy of Switzerland *Commissum divinitus* (17 May 1835), § 4: "The Church has, by its divine institution, the power of the magisterium to teach and define matters of faith and morals and to interpret the Holy Scriptures without danger of error" (PE, vol. 1, 254).

legitimately exercise it within the Church speak with the authority of Christ and in his name, who said to the apostles: "He that hears you hears me: and he that despises you despises me: and he that despises me despises him that sent me" (Lk 10:16). As the Second Vatican Council teaches, the bishops of the Church "are the authentic teachers, that is, teachers endowed with the authority of Christ, who preach to the people entrusted to them the faith to be believed (*fidem credendam*) and put into practice (*et moribus applicandam*)."[13]

As a power, namely the power to teach authoritatively in the name of Christ, the magisterium must be rooted in a subject with a proper act ordered toward a specific object. Moreover, each is twofold: the subject of the magisterium can be either the pope or the bishops (which still includes the pope); the object of the magisterium can be divinely revealed truths of faith or morals (dogmas) or other truths closely connected with these (doctrines); the act of the magisterium can be either ordinary (teaching) or extraordinary (judging); and the power or authority of the magisterium can be either universal or particular.

This work is principally concerned with the pope alone as subject of the magisterium and only insofar as he exercises a universal power. The first distinction is clear: we focus on the magisterium exercised by the pope rather than by any or all of the other bishops of the Church. But further distinctions can then be made with regard to the pope himself. The first such is between the pope as a private and as a public person. Catholic doctrine does not attribute infallibility to the pope as a private person, although this has been held by some theologians, and St Robert Bellarmine calls it a pious and probable opinion.[14] As a public person, a further

---

[13] Vatican II, *Lumen gentium*, § 25: "Episcopi enim sunt fidei praecones, qui novos discipulos ad Christum adducunt, et doctores authentici seu auctoritate Christi praediti, qui populo sibi commisso fidem credendam et moribus applicandam praedicant." (DEC, 869).

[14] St Robert Bellarmine, S.J., *De controversiis christianae fidei adversus hujus temporis haereticos: Tertia controversia generalis: De summo pontifice*, lib. 4, cap. 6: "Probabile est, pieque credi potest, summum pontificem, non solum ut pontificem errare non posse, sed etiam ut particularem personam haereticum esse non posse, falsum aliquid contra fidem pertinaciter credendo" (*Opera omnia*, vol. 1, ed. Xisto Riario Sforza [Naples: Giuliano, 1856], 484).

distinction is then made between the pope as a temporal ruler and as a spiritual ruler; and with regard to the latter it is only as supreme teacher in matters of faith and morals that he is infallible, not as supreme ruler in matters of discipline and government.[15]

Finally, there is a series of further distinctions to be made within the realm of the pope's spiritual authority in matters of faith and morals based on the scope of his teaching activity. The pope acts with a universal authority when he addresses a teaching to the whole Church, such as now frequently occurs in encyclical letters and other universally promulgated documents. However, when the pope proclaims a teaching only to the clergy or faithful of his own diocese, he acts with the particular authority of the local bishop of the diocese of Rome. Such things as papal allocutions to the cardinals or clergy of Rome, papal sermons, and general audiences addressed to the faithful of the diocese clearly fall into this category. Intermediately, when the pope addresses an encyclical letter only to a particular church or group of churches, he may be acting more precisely as patriarch of the West or primate of Italy.[16]

The most famous defender of this opinion was Albert Pighius. Pious it may be, but I would call it rather doubtful than probable. A contemporary example of a pope teaching as a private scholar is furnished by Joseph Ratzinger (Pope Benedict XVI), *Jesus of Nazareth*, vol. 1, trans. Adrian J. Walker (New York: Doubleday, 2007); vol. 2, trans. Philip J. Whitmore (San Francisco: Ignatius Press, 2011).

[15] Compare the definition of papal infallibility, which speaks of the pope as 'supreme pastor and teacher' defining 'doctrine of faith and morals' (Vatican I, *Pastor Aeternus*, cap. 4) with the broader scope of the pope's supreme jurisdiction defined in cap. 3: "So, then, if anyone says that the Roman pontiff has merely an office of supervision and guidance, and not the full and supreme power of jurisdiction over the whole church, and this not only in matters of faith and morals, but also in those which concern the discipline and government of the church dispersed throughout the whole world; or that he has only the principal part, but not the absolute fullness, of this supreme power; or that this power of his is not ordinary and immediate both over all and each of the churches and over all and each of the pastors and faithful: let him be anathema" (DEC, 814–15).

[16] Although the title 'Patriarch of the West' is no longer used by Pope Benedict XVI, the question remains as to what level of authority the pope employs in doctrinal decisions which regard only another particular church or group of churches in the West. For example, Pope St Pius X's Apostolic Letter *Notre Charge Apostolique* (15 Aug. 1910) is addressed only to the French Bishops – hence, it may be viewed as an exercise of his authority as patriarch of

The definition of papal infallibility at Vatican I only attributes infallibility to acts of the pope as supreme head of the universal Church.[17] The pope is not declared to be infallible as patriarch of the West, primate of Italy, or local bishop of Rome. At the same time, however, neither is this positively excluded by the definition, which lacks the word 'only' in its enumeration of the conditions of infallibility. The infallibility of the pope in his capacity as local bishop of the particular Church of Rome (and *a fortiori* as primate of Italy and patriarch of the West) is certainly not a dogma of faith, nor even a Catholic doctrine, but it can be held as a free theological opinion, and indeed, there are strong arguments in its favor which can be drawn from the doctrine of the inerrancy of the particular Church of the city of Rome.[18] Nevertheless, leaving this question aside, it should be understood that this work treats of the pope only in his capacity as supreme shepherd and teacher of the universal Church acting in relation to the universal Church. Presupposing this as the adequate subject of papal infallibility, our present investigation inquires into the extension of the infallibility of the papal magisterium with respect to its object and to its act. In method the work is partly positive and partly speculative. That is, I seek both to establish what the doctrine of the Church is and to

---

the West; Pope Benedict XIV's Encyclical Letter on Usury and Other Dishonest Profit *Vix pervenit* (1 Nov. 1745) is addressed to the Bishops of Italy, and may therefore be considered an act of the pope as primate of Italy.

[17] Thus Patrick Toner, "Infallibility," in CE, 7:796: "Infallibility is not attributed to every doctrinal act of the pope. . . . The pontiff must teach in his public and official capacity as pastor and doctor of all Christians, not merely in his private capacity as a theologian, preacher or allocutionist, nor in his capacity as a temporal prince or as a mere ordinary of the Diocese of Rome. It must be clear that he speaks as spiritual head of the Church universal."

[18] That "the Church of the city of Rome can err" has been formally condemned as heretical by Pope Sixtus IV, Bull *Licet ea* (9 Aug. 1479); D 730. The contrary truth appears in the famous *Dictatus papae* of Pope St Gregory VII: "The Roman church has never erred; nor will it err to all eternity, the Scripture bearing witness" (*Dictatus papae*, no. 22, in *Select Historical Documents of the Middle Ages*, ed. and trans. Ernest F. Henderson [London: George Bell, 1903], 367). For discussion of this much neglected topic see Joseph C. Fenton, "The Local Church of Rome," *American Ecclesiastical Review* 122 (1950): 454–64; "The Doctrinal Authority of Papal Allocutions," *American Ecclesiastical Review* 134 (1956): 109–17.

propose arguments with respect to points not yet specifically determined by ecclesiastical authority.

Division of the Work

This work is divided into two parts. Part One takes up the question of the extension of the object of papal infallibility, which is largely a question of the positive interpretation of the First Vatican Council's definition of papal infallibility. Chapter One focuses on the status or theological note of the doctrine of the pope's infallibility with regard to the secondary object of the magisterium, principally by means of a thorough examination of the teaching of the two councils of the Vatican. Chapter Two then treats of the scope or extension of the secondary object itself, with particular reference to specific moral norms of the natural law. This is a central point in the question of dissent from Catholic moral teaching, which has been prominent since the publication of *Humanae vitae* in 1968.

Part Two then turns to the ordinary and extraordinary modes of exercise of the papal magisterium. Chapter Three proposes speculative argumentation for the infallibility of the ordinary magisterium of the pope. This is a question which was discussed much in the period between the Vatican councils but has all but vanished from theological discourse since the 1960s. Chapter Four takes up the same question from the point of view of positive magisterial teaching, specifically inquiring as to whether the infallibility of the ordinary papal magisterium is actually included in the definition of Vatican I. The very interesting and somewhat controversial cases of *Ordinatio sacerdotalis* (1994) and *Evangelium vitae* (1995) are examined in light of this question, and the chapter then concludes with a review of some of the historical instances of infallible papal teaching.

My principal interlocutor throughout the work will be the distinguished Jesuit theologian Francis A. Sullivan. Professor of ecclesiology for more than three decades at the Gregorian University in Rome, Sullivan has contributed numerous scholarly articles on the subjects under discussion here. He is widely regarded as one of the foremost authorities on the nature and functioning of the magisterium, and is the author of what is perhaps the most influential basic text on the magisterium written in the English language.[19]

---

[19] Francis A. Sullivan, S.J., *Magisterium: Teaching Authority in the Catholic Church* (New York; Ramsey, N.J.: Paulist Press, 1983). This book has been widely used as a basic text in schools and seminaries, and according to Cardinal Dulles it remains "the standard book in English" on the subject (Avery Dulles, S.J., *Magisterium: Teacher and Guardian of the Faith* [Naples, Fl.: Sapientia Press, 2007], 2, n. 3). Anthony J. Figueiredo considers Richard McCormick together with Sullivan and Dulles as the most prominent American authorities on the magisterium in his dissertation, *The Magisterium-Theology Relationship: Contemporary Theological Conceptions in the Light of Universal Church Teaching since 1835 and the Pronouncements of the Bishops of the United States* (Rome: Gregorian University Press, 2001).

PART I.
THE PRIMARY AND SECONDARY OBJECT OF PAPAL INFALLIBILITY

CHAPTER ONE

THE TEACHING OF
VATICAN I AND VATICAN II

The primary object of the magisterium is divinely revealed truth, both speculative (faith) and practical (morals); secondarily, the object of the magisterium encompasses every other truth pertaining to faith or morals which, although not divinely revealed, are nevertheless so intimately connected with divine revelation that their denial would undermine in some way the deposit of faith. Commonly held examples of truths belonging to the secondary object of the magisterium include theological conclusions (derived from premises of which one is divinely revealed and the other only naturally certain), dogmatic facts (e.g. the legitimacy of a papal election or an ecumenical council), particular truths of reason which are intrinsically connected with divine revelation (e.g. the nature of personhood, substantial and accidental being, hylomorphism, etc.), the final approbation of religious orders, and the canonization of saints.[1]

At the First Vatican Council the object of papal infallibility was defined as 'doctrine of faith or morals'. The question at hand is how to interpret this with regard to the secondary object of the magisterium. It is clear that if it means anything at all it declares at least the primary object of the magisterium to be an adequate object of infallible teaching; but does it include, exclude, or simply

---

[1] Cf. Ott, *Fundamentals of Catholic Dogma*, 8–9; 299; Joseph C. Fenton, "The Question of Ecclesiastical Faith," *American Ecclesiastical Review* 128 (1953): 288.

leave open the question of infallibility with respect to the secondary object?

a) The Drafting of the Vatican Definition

The successive drafts of the definition of papal infallibility throughout the course of the First Vatican Council provide a first indication that the formulation of the object of infallibility as 'doctrine of faith or morals' was intended by the fathers of the council to be understood broadly as inclusive of secondary truths of Catholic doctrine pertaining to faith or morals. The drafting of the definition of the infallibility of the papal magisterium took place in three stages.

A first draft was prepared by the theological commission prior to the council in case the question should arise. When it was introduced at the request of the majority of the bishops, this text was distributed and the bishops were invited to submit their written observations on it to the deputation *de fide*, which was entrusted with the drafting of the definition during the council. The deputation, which was composed of bishops elected by their brethren at the council, then prepared a revised draft to serve as the basis of discussion in the council hall. After the closure of the conciliar debate, the draft returned to the deputation for further revision. Among some fifty proposals for an amended formula of the definition, one was selected by the deputation, and this third draft was presented to the bishops, voted upon again, and then finally promulgated on July 18, 1870.

The most important changes which can be noted from one draft to the next concern precisely the extension of the object of papal infallibility. The initial draft of the theological commission describes the object of infallible papal definitions as: "What in things of faith and morals is to be held by the universal Church" (*quid in rebus fidei et morum ab universa Ecclesia tenendum sit*).[2]

---

[2] The Latin text of the draft is provided by Theodor Granderath, S.J., *Geschichte des Vatikanischen Konzils: von seiner ersten Ankündigung bis zu seiner Vertagung: nach den authentischen Dokumenten*, ed. Konrad Kirch, S.J. (Freiburg: Herder, 1903–1906), 3:123: "Definimus per divinam assistentiam fieri, ut Romanus Pontifex . . . cum supremi omnium Christianorum doctoris munere fungens pro auctoritate definit, quid in rebus fidei et morum ab universa

16

The second draft, prepared by the deputation, inserted an additional qualification: "What in things of faith and morals is to be held by the universal Church by divine faith or to be rejected as contrary to the (same) faith" (*quid in rebus fidei et morum ab universa Ecclesia fide divina tenendum vel tamquam [eidem] fidei contrarium reiiciendum sit*).[3]

A note from the diary of Ignatius von Senestréy, the Bishop of Regensburg and a member of the deputation *de fide*, explains the significance of this change, and how it came about. He notes that Cardinal Bilio, the president of the deputation, criticized the first draft at a meeting on May 5, 1870, arguing:

> "No more can be defined concerning the infallibility of the Pope than has been defined concerning the infallibility of the Church; but of the Church this only is of faith, that she is infallible in dogmatic definitions strictly taken; therefore the question arises whether in the proposed formula the infallibility of the Pope be not too widely extended."[4]

The problem concerned the precise theological note or qualification to be assigned to distinct propositions. The practice of theological notation involves two basic considerations, namely, divine revelation and ecclesiastical proposition.

With regard to divine revelation, there are first of all doctrines of faith or morals which are immediately revealed by God, that is, contained in the deposit of faith, whether written

---

Ecclesia tenendum sit, errare non possit; et hanc Romani Pontificis inerrantiae seu infallibilitatis praerogativam ad idem obiectum porrigi, ad quod infallibilitatis Ecclesiae extenditur."

[3] Granderath, *Geschichte des Vatikanischen Konzils*, 3:125: "Declaramus Romanum Pontificem . . . vi divinae promissionis et assistentiae Spiritus Sancti errare non posse, cum supremi omnium Christianorum doctoris munere fungens pro Apostolica sua auctoritate definit, quid in rebus fidei et morum ab universa Ecclesia *fide divina* tenendum vel tamquam *(eidem) fidei* contrarium reiiciendum sit. . . . Porro cum una eademque sit Ecclesiae infallibilitas, sive spectetur in capite Ecclesiae sive in universa Ecclesia docente cum capite unita, *hanc (unam) infallibilitatem etiam ad unum idemque obiectum sese extendere docemus.*"

[4] The entry from Senestréy's diary is recorded in Msi, 53:276–86. The English translation is provided by Cuthbert Butler, O.S.B., *The Vatican Council: The Story Told from Inside in Bishop Ullathorne's Letters* (London; New York; Toronto: Longmans, Green and Co., 1930), 2:123.

(Scripture) or handed down (Tradition); such divinely revealed truths are at least materially dogmas of divine faith (*de fide divina*). This constitutes the primary object of the magisterium. Secondly, there are truths which are logically or historically connected with divine revelation in such a way that their denial would undermine the deposit of faith. The truth of these doctrines, which belong to the secondary object of the magisterium, is guaranteed by their close connection with divine revelation, on account of which they are called theologically certain (*theologice certum*). Beyond this are matters not strictly connected with divine revelation, which are only more or less probable from the point of view of theology.[5]

To this consideration of divine revelation may then be added that of ecclesiastical proposition. Doctrines of faith or morals which are divinely revealed, and which are explicitly proposed as such by the Church, are dogmas in the strict sense; they are to be believed with divine and Catholic faith (*de fide divina et catholica credenda*).[6] Divine or theological faith is based on the authority of God revealing; Catholic or ecclesiastical faith relies on the authority of the Church teaching. A proposition contrary to a dogma is of itself heretical; obstinate doubt or denial of a dogma by the baptized constitutes the sin of heresy.[7]

Secondly, the Church may propose a doctrine of faith or morals as certainly true on account of its being at least intimately connected with divine revelation. These may be called truths of Catholic doctrine, or simply Catholic doctrines; they are to be held

---

[5] This is not to say, of course, that the genuine conclusions of philosophy or other human sciences do not attain to certitude, but only that their certitude is not theological in character.

[6] Vatican Council I, Session III, Dogmatic Constitution on the Catholic Faith *Dei Filius* (24 Apr. 1870), cap. 3: "Wherefore, by divine and Catholic faith all those things are to be believed which are contained in the word of God as found in scripture and tradition, and which are proposed by the Church as matters to be believed as divinely revealed, whether by her solemn judgment or in her ordinary and universal magisterium" (DEC, 807).

[7] *Code of Canon Law* (1983), can. 751: "Heresy is the obstinate denial or obstinate doubt after the reception of baptism of some truth which is to be believed by divine and Catholic faith." Cf. can. 1364 § 1: Without prejudice to the prescript of can. 194, § 1, n. 2, an apostate from the faith, a heretic, or a schismatic incurs a latae sententiae excommunication; in addition, a cleric can be punished with the penalties mentioned in can. 1336, § 1, nn. 1, 2, and 3."

definitively with Catholic or ecclesiastical faith (*de fide definitive tenenda*). Their rejection falls under the censure of error, but not of heresy.[8] It should be noted that some truths of Catholic doctrine may be materially contained in divine revelation, although they have not yet been explicitly proposed as divinely revealed. Such was the status, for example, of the doctrine of papal infallibility prior to its definition as a dogma in 1870.[9]

Beyond these categories lies the realm of free theological opinion on matters connected with faith and morals which are neither evident on the basis of divine revelation nor determined by the Church. These can range from tolerated opinions (*opinio tolerata*) to probable, more probable, and well founded judgments (*sententia probabilis*, *probabilior*, *bene fundata*). If theologians are generally agreed upon the truth of a particular theological opinion it is a common teaching (*sententia communis*), to depart from which without reason would justly be censured as temerarious (*propositio temeraria*).[10]

To return, then, to the problem posed by Cardinal Bilio in the meeting of the deputation *de fide*, it was clear that the infallibility of the Church in defining dogmas was itself a dogma to be held by divine and Catholic faith. That the Church was likewise infallible in her merely doctrinal (non-dogmatic) definitions was held to be certainly true and at least intimately connected with

---

[8] *Code of Canon Law* (1983), can. 750, § 2: "one who rejects those propositions which are to be held definitively is opposed to the doctrine of the Catholic Church." Cf. can. 1371: "The following are to be punished with a just penalty: 1/ in addition to the case mentioned in can. 1364, § 1, a person who teaches a doctrine condemned by the Roman Pontiff or by an ecumenical council or who obstinately rejects the doctrine mentioned in can. 750, § 2 or in can. 752 and who does not retract after having been admonished by the Apostolic See or an ordinary." Cf. Congregation for the Doctrine of the Faith, Doctrinal Commentary on the Concluding Formula of the *Professio fidei* (29 Jun. 1998), § 6: "Every believer, therefore, is required to give firm and definitive assent to these truths, based on faith in the Holy Spirit's assistance to the Church's Magisterium, and on the Catholic doctrine of the infallibility of the Magisterium in these matters. Whoever denies these truths would be in a position of *rejecting a truth of Catholic doctrine and would therefore no longer be in full communion with the Catholic Church.*"

[9] Cf. CDF, *Doctrinal Commentary*, § 11.

[10] Cf. Ott, *Fundamentals of Catholic Dogma*, 4–10.

divine revelation, but it had not been settled whether this was immediately revealed by God or merely theologically certain. Cardinal Bilio's point was that the solution of this question should not be pre-empted by the definition of papal infallibility; therefore the infallibility of the pope should be defined only as extending to divinely revealed dogmas.

THEOLOGICAL NOTATION		Ecclesiastical Proposition		
		Explicitly proposed as	Implicitly proposed as	Not proposed as
Divine Revelation	Divinely revealed:	*Dogma*	*Proximate to Faith*	*N / A*
	Theologically certain:	*Truth of Catholic Doctrine*	*Pertaining to Faith*	*Theologically Certain*
	Theologically probable:	*Authentic Catholic Teaching*	*Theologically Probable*	*Theologically Probable*

For the Cardinal, at least, it was clear that the formulation of the object of papal infallibility as 'things of faith and morals to be held by the universal Church' would include secondary truths of Catholic doctrine; therefore he insisted on the addition of the words 'by divine faith' (*fide divina*) which clearly excludes them, for only divinely revealed dogmas are held by divine faith: secondary truths of Catholic doctrine are held by Catholic or ecclesiastical faith. The counter-argument reported by Senestréy was that this formula would be widely misinterpreted as not only a non-affirmation of papal infallibility with regard to secondary truths of Catholic doctrine, but rather as a positive denial of it. Taken together with the clause equating the infallibility of the pope with that of the Church, this would then also be taken to mean that the Church herself had been positively declared to be fallible in such matters. Cardinal Bilio's arguments prevailed in the deputation, however, and the revised draft with the restricted object was distributed to the bishops.

Nevertheless, in the final draft, which was ultimately approved and promulgated by the council, the crucial qualification 'by divine faith' (*fide divina*) was removed. The object was again said to be simply "doctrine of faith or morals to be held by the universal Church" (*doctrinam de fide vel moribus ab universa Ecclesia tenendam*).[11] That the council fathers ultimately rejected a formulation which restricted the object of papal infallibility to divinely revealed dogmas, in favor of a broader formulation, is in itself a clear indication that the phrase 'doctrine of faith or morals' in the final definition is intended to be understood as including secondary truths of Catholic doctrine. At the same time, it must be noted that the definition does not simply declare it to be a dogma that the pope's merely doctrinal definitions are infallible, but rather that he enjoys the same infallibility which the Church enjoys in defining doctrine of faith and morals.

b) The Explanations of Bishop Gasser

The thorough explanation of this carefully nuanced formulation delivered by Bishop Gasser is of unique importance here. His was the task of introducing and explaining the third and final draft of the definition to the council as the official representative of the deputation *de fide*. There is much that is of great interest in Gasser's 'relatio' of July 11, 1870, which lasted nearly four hours, but especially valuable are his explanations of the formulation of the object of papal infallibility.[12]

---

[11] Granderath, *Geschichte des Vatikanischen Konzils*, 3:474: "Romanum Pontificem, cum ex cathedra loquitur, id est, cum omnium Christianorum pastoris et doctoris munere fungens, pro suprema sua Apostolica auctoritate doctrinam de fide vel moribus ab universa Ecclesia tenendam definit, per assistentiam divinam, ipsi in beato Petro promissam, ea infallibilitate pollere, qua divinus Redemptor Ecclesiam suam in definienda doctrina de fide vel moribus instructam esse voluit, ideoque eiusmodi Romani Pontificis definitiones esse ex sese irreformabilis." The essential portion of each of the three drafts are presented together in English translation by Butler, *The Vatican Council*, 2:133.

[12] The entire text of Gasser's speech of June 11, 1870 appears in Msi, 52:1204–30; it has been translated into English with commentary by O'Connor

When Gasser comes to the object of papal infallibility he begins by reminding his audience that the purpose of infallibility is "to guard and unfold the integral deposit of faith."[13] He continues: "From this it can easily be seen that, in general, the object of infallibility is doctrine about faith and morals. But not all truths which pertain to the doctrine of faith and Christian morals are of the same kind."[14] The phrase 'doctrine of faith and morals' is generic, embracing within itself various kinds of doctrines, which are specified by the nature of their relationship to the deposit of faith; but it should be noted that Gasser refers the gift of infallibility immediately to the entire genus. He then makes three points about the way in which infallibility pertains to different classes of doctrine. First of all, he says:

> "It is certain that the infallibility promised by God completely includes the same extent of truths whether that infallibility resides in the whole Church teaching, when it defines truths in council, or in the supreme Pontiff considered in himself. This is so since the purpose of infallibility is the same in whichever mode it is exercised."[15]

His second point is that there can be no doubt that the divinely revealed promise of infallibility (whether exercised by the pope alone or by the bishops together) includes the fact that it extends at least to divinely revealed truths:

> "Hence it clearly is believed and must be believed as a matter of faith by all the children of holy Mother Church that the Church is infallible

---

in *The Gift of Infallibility*, 19–91; Butler devotes a chapter to Gasser's exposition in *The Vatican Council*, 2:134–48; as does Granderath, *Geschichte des Vatikanischen Konzils*, 3:455–77.

[13] Gasser, *The Gift of Infallibility*, 75: "Infallibilitas promissa est ad custodiendum et evolvendum integrum depositum fidei" (Msi, 52:1225).

[14] Ibid.: "Hinc universim quidem facile patet, obiectum infallibilitatis esse doctrinam de fide et moribus. At non omnes veritates, quae ad doctrinam de fide et moribus christianis pertinent, sunt unius modi; nec omnes in uno eodemque gradu ad custodiam integritatis depositi necessariae sunt" (Msi, 52:1225).

[15] Ibid.: "Iam . . . certum est, infallibilitatem a Deo promissam, sive in tota ecclesia docente, cum in concilia veritates definit, sive in ipso summo pontifice . . . ad eundem omnino ambitum veritatum extendi; cum idem sit finis infallibilitatis, utrovie modo ea consideretur" (Msi, 52:1226).

in proposing and defining dogmas of faith. Now in the same manner, the infallibility of the head of the Church is not able to be revealed and defined unless, by that very fact, it is revealed and defined that the Pontiff is infallible in defining dogmas of faith."[16]

Gasser's third point then addresses the truths which fall under the secondary object of the magisterium. "Together with revealed truths, there are," he says, "other truths more or less strictly connected. These truths, although they are not revealed *in se*, are nevertheless required in order to guard fully, explain properly and define efficaciously the very deposit of faith."[17] Gasser proceeds to explain the problem to which we have already seen Cardinal Bilio refer in the course of drafting the definition:

> "All Catholic theologians completely agree that the Church, in her authentic proposal and definition of truths of this sort, is infallible, such that to deny this infallibility would be a very grave error. A diversity of opinion turns only on the question of the degree of certitude, i.e., on whether the infallibility in proposing these truths – and therefore in proscribing errors through censures inferior to the note of heresy – should be considered a dogma of faith, so that to deny this infallibility to the Church would be heretical, or whether it is a truth not revealed in itself but one deduced from revealed dogma and as such is only theologically certain."[18]

---

[16] Ibid., 76: "Hinc sane de fide creditur et credendum est ab omnibus filiis matris ecclesiae, ecclesiam in proponendis ac definiendis dogmatibus fidei infallibilem esse. Eodem autem modo infallibilitas capitis ecclesiae revelata esse et definiri non poterit, quin eo ipso revelatum sit ac definiatur pontificem esse infallibilem in definiendis fidei dogmatibus" (Msi, 52:1226).

[17] Gasser, *The Gift of Infallibility*, 76: "At vero cum dogmatibus revelatis, ut . . . ante dixi, veritates alias magis vel minus stricte cohaerent, quae licit in se revelatae non sint, requiruntur tamen ad ipsum depositum revelationis integre custodiendum, rite explicandum et efficaciter definiendum" (Msi, 52:1226).

[18] Ibid.: "Hinc omnes omnino catholici theologi consentiunt, ecclesiam in huiusmodi veritatum authentica propositione ac definitione esse infallibilem, ita ut hanc infallibilitatem negare gravissimus esset error. Sed opinionum diversitas versatur unice circa gradum certitudinis, utrum scilicet infallibilitas in hisce veritatibus proponendis, ac proinde in erroribus per censuras nota haereseos inferiores proscribendis debeat conseri dogma fidei, ut hanc infallibilitatem ecclesiae negans esset haereticus; an solum sit veritas in se non revelata, sed ex revelata dogmata deducta, ac proinde solum theologice certa" (Msi, 52:1226).

Since the same must be said of the infallibility of the pope as of the infallibility of the whole Church, the problem arises as to how to define the extension of the papal infallibility with the proper theological note. It is agreed that the pope is infallible in dogmatic definitions, and that this is divinely revealed; it is agreed that the pope is infallible in merely doctrinal (non-dogmatic) definitions, but it is unclear whether this is divinely revealed or merely theologically certain. Having decided that it would be better not to settle this question, but to leave theologians free to discuss it, the deputation proposed a solution which would define the truth of papal infallibility generically, while leaving open the question of which theological note should be applied in the specific case. Gasser explains:

> "Thus, the present definition about the object of infallibility contains two parts which are intimately connected. The first part enunciates the object of infallibility only generically, namely that it is doctrine of faith and morals. The second part of the definition distinctly sets forth this object of infallibility, not indeed by individual considerations, but by circumscribing and determining it by comparing it with the infallibility of the Church in defining, so that the very same thing must be confessed about the object of infallibility when the Pope is defining as must be confessed about the object of infallibility when the Church is defining."[19]

The force of Gasser's explanation of this carefully formulated definition of the object of papal infallibility consists in these three points: (1) it is true that the infallibility of the pope extends generically to all doctrine of faith and morals; (2) it is a divinely revealed truth that the infallibility of the pope extends specifically to divinely revealed truths; and (3) it is at least theologically certain that the infallibility of the pope extends to non-revealed truths which nevertheless pertain in some degree to the deposit of

---

[19] Gasser, *The Gift of Infallibility*, 77: "Hinc praesens definitio de obiecto infallibilitatis duas continet partes inter se intime nexas. Pars prior obiectum infallibilitatis solum generice enunciat, illud nempe esse doctrinam de fide et moribus; pars vero altera noc obiectum non quidem per singula distincto declarat, sed illud circumscribit ac determinat per comparationem cum infallibilitate in definitionibus ecclesiae, adeo ut omnino idem profitendum sit de obiecto infallibilitatis in definitionibus editis a pontifice, quod profitendum est de obiecto infallibilitatis in definitionibus ecclesiae" (Msi, 52:1226–27).

faith. The definition includes and expresses each of these three points.

After Gasser's lengthy introduction to the new formulation of the definition, a vote was taken two days later, which allowed the bishops to vote *'placet'* ('it pleases'), *'non placet'* ('it does not please'), or *'placet iuxta modum'* ('it pleases in a way', that is, with certain reservations). Those who voted *'placet iuxta modum'* were required to submit their reservations or suggestions for alterations in writing to the deputation *de fide*. Then, on July 16, Bishop Gasser again took to the floor in order to explain why some of these proposed emendations had been rejected by the deputation while others were proposed for the council to vote upon. It was at this point that the title of the fourth chapter of the constitution was changed from 'on the infallibility of the pope' to 'on the infallible magisterium of the pope' in order to preclude the misconception that the pope was being declared impeccable. The final clause rejecting the necessity of the consent of the Church as a condition of the irreformability of papal definitions was also added against the Gallican doctrine. And Gasser again had to clarify the import of the definition on the object of papal infallibility, this time in connection with the word 'defines' (*definit*).

Some of the council fathers were afraid that the word 'defines' would be construed as limiting papal infallibility to dogmatic definitions. Hence alternative words such as 'decree' were proposed instead. In response to this Gasser explains:

> "Indeed, the Deputation *de fide* is not of the mind that this word should be understood in a juridical sense (Lat. *in sensu forensi*) so that it only signifies putting an end to controversy which has arisen in respect to heresy and doctrine which is properly speaking *de fide*. Rather, the word 'defines' signifies that the Pope directly and conclusively pronounces his sentence about a doctrine which concerns matters of faith or morals and does so in such a way that each one of the faithful can be certain of the mind of the Apostolic See, of the mind of the Roman Pontiff; in such a way, indeed, that he or she knows for certain that such and such a doctrine is held to be heretical, proximate to heresy, certain or erroneous, etc., by the Roman Pontiff."[20]

---

[20] Gasser, *The Gift of Infallibility*, 74: "Utique Deputatio de fide non in ea mente est, quod verbum istud debeat sumi in sensu forensi, ut solummodo significet finem impositum controversiae, quae de haeresi et de doctrina quae

The main point here again is that, like the formulation 'doctrine of faith or morals', the word 'defines' is intended to be understood generically as embracing not only divinely revealed truths and condemnations of heresy, but also secondary truths of Catholic doctrine which correspond to censures less than heresy.

The question left open by the council is not, as has too frequently been assumed, whether or not the pope is infallible in his merely doctrinal definitions. By its generic formulation of the object, the council declares that he is, although it avoids qualifying this as a dogma. The only question left open is whether or not this truth is revealed by God. It may or may not be a material dogma, but it is in any case a theologically certain truth of Catholic doctrine, which is to be held definitively by Catholic or ecclesiastical faith (*de fide definitive tenenda*). Confusion on this point arises from the fact that Gasser says that the question about the extension of infallibility to the secondary object "should be left in the state in which it presently is,"[21] that is, as a doctrine which is at least theologically certain. The problem is that it then becomes very easy to impose one's own understanding of the meaning of 'theologically certain', thereby determining also the present theological qualification of the doctrine.

If one simply looks up the meaning of the note 'theologically certain' in the manuals of dogmatic theology, one will find some systems of notation wherein this note includes a lack of definitive ecclesiastical proposition, such as in Ott's *Fundamentals of Catholic Dogma*: "A doctrine, on which the Teaching Authority of the Church has not yet finally pronounced,

---

proprie est de fide, agitata fuit; sed vox *definit* significat, quod papa suam sententiam circa doctrinam, quae est de rebus fidei et morum, directe et terminative proferat, ita ut iam unusquisque fidelium certus esse possit de mente sedis apostolicae, de mente Romani pontificis; ita quidem ut certo sciat a Romano pontifice hanc vel illam doctrinam haberi haereticam, haeresi proximam, certam vel erroneam, etc." (Msi, 52:1316).

[21] Gasser, *The Gift of Infallibility*, 77: "Cum autem patribus Deputationis unanimi consensione visum sit hanc quaestionem nunc saltem non definiendam, sed reliquendam esse in eo statu in quo est . . ." (Msi, 52:1226). This statement has received inordinate attention from some authors who have drawn from it the conclusion that the infallibility of the Church with regard to the secondary object remained a matter of free theological opinion even after the council.

but whose truth is guaranteed by its intrinsic connection with the doctrine of revelation (theological conclusions)."[22] Other systems, such as that prepared by Sixtus Cartechini for the use of the Holy Office, use the note to mean, positively, that the proposition is certain in itself, and negatively, that it has not been proposed by the Church as a revealed dogma of faith.[23] This does not exclude that the doctrine has been definitively proposed by the Church as a theologically certain truth, but only as a divinely revealed truth. Hence some caution must be exercised in interpreting Gasser's meaning.

The decisive point is to realize that Gasser is not concerned in the least with the category of ecclesiastical proposition, but only with divine revelation. He speaks always about the problem as to whether the doctrine is revealed by God or merely theologically certain, and never at all about whether or not it has been sufficiently proposed by the Church. From his own words, the only meaning attached to the note 'theologically certain' is: "A truth not revealed in itself but one deduced from revealed dogma."[24] He speaks only of the secondary object of the magisterium as distinct from the primary object, without any reference to ecclesiastical proposition. Thus he uses the note 'theologically certain' as Cartechini does, rather than like Ott; and so Francis Sullivan is mistaken when he essentially downgrades the doctrine to a common teaching (*sententia communis*) by admitting only that it is "held by most Catholic theologians to be certain."[25] The implication of Sullivan's position is that the doctrine would still fall within the field of free theological opinion, from which dissent is in principle permissible.

---

[22] Ott, *Fundamentals of Catholic Dogma*, 9–10.

[23] Sixtus Cartechini, S.J., *De valore notarum theologicarum et de criteriis ad eas dignoscendas* (Rome: Gregorian University Press, 1951), I, cap. 11: "Duo elementa definiunt quaenam sit propositio theologice certa: unum positivum, aliud negativum. Positivum est certitudo veritatis ipsius propositionis theologice certae, quae certitudo habetur ex universalitate consensus ut in propositionem theologice certam, vel saltem ex intimo nexu cum doctrina fidei. Negativum est quod ista propositio non proponitur et praedicatur ut certo revelata ac de fide."

[24] Gasser, *The Gift of Infallibility*, 76; cited above, p. 21, n. 18.

[25] Sullivan, *Magisterium*, 133–34.

To return to Gasser's point, the state of the question indeed remains unchanged; but which question? Not the question of ecclesiastical proposition, but only the question of divine revelation of which Gasser actually speaks: the question of whether the teaching belongs to the primary or secondary object of the magisterium. Only this adequately explains how the state of the question remains unchanged when it is everywhere equally clear that the council does propose that the infallibility of the pope reaches to the entire genus of faith and morals.[26]

c) The Interpretation of Bishop Fessler

Perhaps the most influential interpreter of the definition after the council was Joseph Fessler, Bishop of Sankt Pölten in Austria, who acted as General Secretary at the First Vatican Council. His was the task of defending the council and the definition against the attacks of the 'Old Catholics'.[27] Opposition to the definition of papal infallibility had been ongoing since before the council had convened. It arose primarily from the threat to political and ecclesiastical liberalism posed by the recently published *Syllabus of Errors*, and the Encyclical Letter *Quanta cura* (1864) to which this was appended, as well as by the more ancient Bull *Unam sanctam* (1302). One of the most prominent 'Old Catholic' writers was Johann Friedrich von Schulte, Professor of Canon and German Law at the University of Prague, and it was against his attack that Bishop Fessler directed his defense of papal infallibility.[28]

---

[26] Alternatively, one could argue that the infallibility of the Church with regard to the secondary object of the magisterium had already been sufficiently proposed, perhaps by the ordinary and universal magisterium of the bishops dispersed throughout the world; in any case the conclusion would remain the same, namely, that the doctrine has been proposed by the Church.

[27] The 'Old Catholic' schism was initiated in September 1870 by the formal rejection of the dogma of infallibility issued by about fourteen hundred Germanic Catholics. For a brief introduction, see Paul M. Baumgarten, "Old Catholics," in CE, 11:235–36; Peter Neuner et al., "Altkatholische Kirchen," in LThK[3], 1:468–71.

[28] The title of Schulte's pamphlet, as recorded by Fessler, is *Die Macht der römischen Päpste über Fürsten, Länder, Völker, Individuen, nach ihren Lehren und Handlungen zur Würdigung ihren Unfehlbarkeit beleuchtet.* Fessler's response was entitled *Die wahre und die falsche Unfehlbarkeit der*

Schulte's stated intention in the pamphlet was to investigate "what is the doctrine of the Church in respect to the relations between the spiritual and temporal power" so that "governments and persons governed may be thoroughly acquainted with what a Catholic who admits the Infallibility of the Pope is bound to believe as matter of conscience."[29] The author hoped to dissuade men from accepting the Vatican definition by means of a *reductio ad absurdum*: if one accepts the Vatican definition, one will have to accept this and that '*ex cathedra*' definition from the medieval popes, or from the *Syllabus of Errors*; implicit is the assumption that modern men can not or will not accept the socio-political doctrines contained therein; the conclusion then follows that they should not accept the definition of papal infallibility.

Fessler's line of defense is simply to deny that any one of Schulte's examples, with the partial exception of *Unam sanctam*, constitutes a definition '*ex cathedra*' according to the sense of the Vatican definition. Fessler begins by restricting the application of the pope's infallibility to two of the four areas in which the pope possesses supreme power of jurisdiction, as defined in the previous chapter of the same constitution.[30] It is with regard to matters of faith and morals that the pope is declared infallible, not with regard to matters of discipline and government. Many of the examples which Schulte dredges up clearly pertain to the latter, or even to the actions of the popes as temporal heads of state, and Fessler is right to dismiss them from consideration.[31]

Päpste: zur Abwehr gegen Hrn. Prof. Dr. Schulte (Vienna: Sartori, 1871). It was soon translated into English as *The True and the False Infallibility of the Popes: A Controversial Reply to Dr. Schulte*, 3rd ed., trans. Ambrose St. John (London: Burns and Oates, 1875).

[29] Fessler, *The True and the False Infallibility*, 54.

[30] Fessler, *The True and the False Infallibility*, 44; cf. Vatican I, *Pastor Aeternus*, cap. 3.

[31] For example, Schulte's fourth 'infallible' proposition is: "The Pope has the right to bestow upon Catholic rulers lands and peoples who are not Catholic, and rulers so made may make them slaves" (cited in Fessler, *The True and the False Infallibility*, 81). This he draws from the fact that Pope Nicholas V, Bull *Romanus Pontifex* (8 Jan. 1454), gave leave to King Alphonsus of Portugal to take possession of Western Africa.

When Fessler discusses the object of infallible definitions more closely, however, he limits it not only to matters of faith and morals in general, but to divinely revealed dogmas of faith and morals in particular. In his discussion of the *Syllabus of Errors*, Fessler argues that none of its condemnations can be considered infallible since it is not specified whether any proposition is condemned precisely as heretical, which alone would be equivalent to declaring its contrary a divinely revealed dogma. First, he offers his interpretation of the extension of infallibility according to the new definition:

> "The condemnation of errors, according to the traditional practice of the Church, is made in various forms: sometimes they are condemned as heretical; sometimes as savouring of heresy; sometimes as schismatic; sometimes simply as erroneous, or false; sometimes as dangerous, or scandalous, or perverse; sometimes as leading to heresy, or to schism, or to disobedience to ecclesiastical superiors. When a particular doctrine has been condemned by the Pope as heretical in the way designated by the doctrinal definition of the Vatican Council, speaking of the Infallible teaching office of the Pope; – then, indeed, there can be no doubt that we have under these circumstances an utterance of the Pope *ex cathedra*."[32]

Then he applies this reasoning to the *Syllabus of Errors*:

> "But as in the Syllabus, through the whole catalogue of eighty propositions, designated generally in the title as 'Errors' (*Syllabus errorum*), there is nothing to show, as was pointed out above, under what category of condemned propositions, according to old ecclesiastical usage, a particular error falls, we are compelled to have recourse to the records or sources, in which the particular propositions of the Syllabus have been on previous occasions condemned by Popes, in order to learn whether it is condemned simply as erroneous, or whether it has some other designation, and notably whether it has been condemned as heretical."[33]

This insistence on divinely revealed dogma, or equivalently on condemnations of heresy, is a recurring point throughout the whole work. The pope has, says Fessler, "The gift of Infallibility,

---

[32] Fessler, *The True and the False Infallibility*, 6.
[33] Ibid., 6–7.

according to the manifest sense of the words of the definition, only as *supreme teacher of truths necessary for salvation revealed by God*."[34] In terms of the object of papal infallibility Fessler is thus three steps removed from Schulte's excessively broad interpretation. Schulte appears to take all matters of faith, morals, discipline, and government, whether temporal or spiritual, to be adequate subject-matter for infallible definitions; Fessler limits the object not only to the spiritual power, and to matters of faith and morals in general, but to divinely revealed dogmas of faith and morals in particular. The actual text of the definition itself, however, especially read in light of Gasser's explanations, stands in between the two controversialists. The infallibility of the pope with respect to the entire genus of faith and morals is taught by the Church in the Vatican definition; it is simply not taught as a dogma in the case of non-dogmatic definitions.

Despite its overly restrictive interpretation of the object of infallibility, Fessler's work received a letter of thanks and approval from Pope Pius IX for his defense of the dogma against the attacks of the 'Old Catholics'.[35] This was understandably taken as a seal of approval upon his interpretation by many authors. Cuthbert Butler, for example, the most prominent historian of the First Vatican Council writing in English, makes much of this "semi-official approbation"[36] of Fessler's interpretation, and represents it as the true interpretation in contrast to the exaggerations of Cardinal Manning, the Archbishop of Westminster who had taken a leading role in promoting the definition of papal infallibility at the council.[37] One comment Butler makes about Manning's interpretation is particularly instructive:

"In the elaborate explanation of the force of the infallibility decree he [Manning] extends its scope so as to include dogmatic facts, censures less than heresy, canonizations of saints, approbations of religious orders: all this is roundly asserted; even though Bishop Gasser, as

---

[34] Ibid., 43; cf. 46, 47, 51, 53, 55.
[35] An extract of the Brief is given in *The True and the False Infallibility*, iii–iv.
[36] Butler, *The Vatican Council*, 2:216.
[37] Ibid.

official spokesman of the deputation *de Fide*, had laid down positively that the theological questions at issue over these matters were not touched by the definition, but were left in the state of theological opinion in which they were before the Council – and still are. In particular, the word 'define' Manning said was to be taken not in a legal but in a large sense, as signifying the final decision by which any matter of faith and morals is put into a doctrinal form."[38]

The appeal to Gasser is especially striking, since it was Gasser himself who had said, as Cardinal Manning well knew, that the word 'define' should not be understood 'in a legal sense' (*in sensu forensi*); on the contrary, he explains it just as Manning does, specifically mentioning censures less than heresy.[39] Butler's claim that Gasser positively asserted that the theological questions at stake regarding secondary truths of Catholic doctrine were not touched by the definition is true, but misleading. As we have seen, the question left untouched was not whether or not the Church is infallible here, but only whether or not this truth belongs to the primary or secondary object of the magisterium. The council left the doctrine in this same state by proposing the truth of the matter without qualifying it as a dogma.

d) Vatican II on the Object of Infallibility

The teaching of the Second Vatican Council with respect to the object of infallible magisterial teaching confirms our interpretation of the First Vatican Council on this point. Vatican II devotes three paragraphs to the charism of infallibility in its Dogmatic Constitution on the Church *Lumen gentium* (1964). Regarding the object of infallibility, the council teaches:

> "This infallibility, however, with which the divine redeemer willed his church to be endowed in defining doctrine concerning faith or morals, extends just as far as the deposit of divine revelation that is to be guarded as sacred and faithfully expounded."[40]

---

[38] Ibid.

[39] Gasser, *The Gift of Infallibility*, 74; cited above, p. 23, n. 20.

[40] Vatican II, *Luman gentium*, § 25: "Haec autem infallibilitas, qua divinus redemptor ecclesiam suam in definienda doctrina de fide vel moribus

32

Some writers have interpreted this to mean that infallibility is positively restricted to the primary object of the magisterium alone, that is, to matters of faith and morals which are formally contained in the deposit of faith.[41] It must be admitted that it would be easy to misread the text in this way, but Sullivan rightly calls attention to the official explanation given to the council fathers by the Theological Commission:

> "The object of the infallibility of the Church thus explained, has the same extension as the revealed deposit; hence it extends to all those things, and only to those, which either directly pertain to the revealed deposit itself, or are required in order that the same deposit may be religiously safeguarded and faithfully expounded."[42]

Whereas Vatican I had only formulated the object of infallibility generically in its definition of papal infallibility, Vatican II, read in light of this official clarification, distinguishes the object into two species, a primary object and a secondary object. The primary object is comprised of all those things which pertain directly to the revealed deposit of faith, that is, to every matter of faith or morals which is formally revealed by God in Scripture or Tradition. The secondary object described here includes every non-revealed truth which is required for defending or expounding revealed truth; these truths pertain indirectly to the deposit of faith.

---

instructam esse voluit, tantum patet quantum divinae revelationis patet depositum, sancte custodiendum et fideliter exponendum" (DEC, 869).

[41] Authors who hold that the magisterium is infallible only with regard to divinely revealed truths include R. S. Prendergast, "Some Neglected Factors of the Birth Control Question," *Sciences Ecclesiastiques* 18 (1966): 218–19; Englebert Gutwenger, S.J., "The Role of the Magisterium," *Concilium* 1.6 (1970): 51; Ludger Oeing-Hanhoff, "Ist das kirchliche Lehramt für den Bereich des Sittlichen zuständig?," *Theologische Quartalschrift* 161 (1981): 56–66; André Naud, *Le magistère incertain* (Montreal: Fides, 1987), 77–96; *Devant la nouvelle profession de foi et le serment de fidélité* (Montreal: Fides, 1989), 43.

[42] AS, III/1, 251: "*Obiectum infallibilitatis* Ecclesiae, ita explicatae, eamdem habet extensionem ac depositum revelatum; ideoque extenditur ad ea omnia, et ad ea tantum, quae vel directe ad ipsum depositum revelatum spectant, vel quae ad idem depositum sancte custodiendum et fideliter exponendum requiruntur, ut habetur in CONC. VAT. I: DENZ. 1836 (3070), ubi de infallibilitate Romani Pontificis." English translation provided by Sullivan, *Magisterium*, 132.

If the relevant text of *Lumen gentium* is to be understood in the way in which it is explained by the Theological Commission which drafted it, then we can make the following observations. The qualification of the doctrine of the Church's infallibility with regard to the secondary object remains unchanged: it is again proposed by an ecumenical council as true, although not specifically as a divinely revealed truth.[43] The scope of the secondary object itself, however, is more fully described here: the secondary object of the magisterium comprises every truth pertaining to faith or morals which is necessary to 'guard inviolate' (*sancte custodiendum*) or to 'expound faithfully' (*fideliter exponendum*) the divinely revealed deposit of faith.

This point will be taken up in greater detail in the next chapter. For the present, it is sufficient to note that our conclusions regarding the teaching of Vatican I are confirmed by the teaching of Vatican II, namely, (1) that the infallibility of the papal magisterium with regard to divinely revealed dogmas of faith or morals is itself a dogma of faith, to be held by divine and Catholic faith (*de fide divina et catholica credenda*); and (2) that the infallibility of the papal magisterium with regard to secondary truths of Catholic doctrine pertaining to faith or morals is itself a truth of Catholic doctrine, to be held definitively by Catholic or ecclesiastical faith (*de fide definitive tenenda*).

---

[43] Noteworthy in this regard is the concluding line of the Theological Commission's explanation, which Sullivan leaves out of his citation. After explaining that the text of *Lumen gentium* does assert the infallibility of the Church with regard to both primary and secondary object, it continues significantly: "as is said in the First Vatican Council, where it speaks of the infallibility of the Roman Pontiff" (my translation; for the Latin text, see n. 42, above).

CHAPTER TWO

SPECIFIC MORAL NORMS
OF THE NATURAL LAW

In the decades following the Second Vatican Council numerous magisterial texts appeared which touched upon the question of the object of the infallible magisterium. The topic of papal infallibility was greatly reinvigorated in theological discussion stemming from Pope Paul VI's condemnation of contraception in the Encyclical Letter *Humanae vitae* (1968). Hans Küng reasoned that this act of teaching fulfilled the conditions for papal infallibility laid down by Vatican I, and so rejected the dogma of papal infallibility, on the grounds that contraception was manifestly good or least morally neutral.[44] Many of the more prominent theologians who disagreed with Küng took issue not with his assessment of the morality of contraception, but rather of the binding authority of the teaching.[45] This was open to question on two fronts: firstly, it appeared as an exercise of the ordinary papal magisterium, the infallible power of which was disputed; and secondly, the doctrine was not manifestly contained in divine revelation, thus opening up a whole new discussion of the adequate object of infallibility.

The decisive question now was not so much whether or not the Church is infallible with regard to the secondary object, but rather, how far does the secondary object itself extend? In particular, does 'doctrine of faith and morals', as the object of infallibility, extend all the way to specific moral norms of the natural law, such as contraception? The opinion of Sullivan,

---

[44] Hans Küng, *Unfehlbar? Eine Anfrage* (Zürich: Benzinger, 1970).

[45] See the discussions in John T. Ford, "Küng on Infallibility: A Review Article," *The Thomist* 35 (1971): 501–12; John J. Hughes, "Infallible? An Inquiry Considered," *Theological Studies* 32 (1971): 183–207.

among many others, is that "such norms are not proper matter for irreformable teaching."[46] The claim that the Church simply cannot teach infallibly about specific moral norms is one of the pillars of contemporary theological dissent from Catholic moral teaching.[47] The question of the extension of infallibility to specific moral norms is fittingly treated in connection with some of the more recent magisterial documents touching upon the subject.

a) CDF: Mysterium Ecclesiae

Less than a decade after the Second Vatican Council, the extension of infallibility to the secondary object was unambiguously asserted in the Declaration *Mysterium Ecclesiae* promulgated in 1973 by the Congregation for the Doctrine of the Faith (CDF). Although not mentioned by name in the document, much of its content clearly refers to the teachings of Hans Küng, who had just published his rejection of the dogma of infallibility on the exact centenary of its promulgation at Vatican I.[48] The Declaration touches upon many points, among which appears an explanation of the primary and secondary object of the infallible magisterium:

> "According to Catholic doctrine, the infallibility of the Church's Magisterium extends not only to the deposit of faith but also to those matters without which that deposit cannot be rightly preserved and expounded. The extension however of this infallibility to the deposit of

---

[46] He continues: "This judgment rules out not only the possibility of the infallible definition of such a norm, but also the claim that such a norm has ever been, or could be, infallibly taught by the ordinary and universal magisterium" (Sullivan, *Magisterium*, 152).

[47] For discussion of this point see, Gerald J. Hughes, "Infallibility in Morals," *Theological Studies* 34 (1973): 415–28; Brian Tierney, "Infallibility in Morals: A Response," *Theological Studies* 35 (1974): 507–17; Germain Grisez, "Infallibility and Specific Moral Norms: A Review Discussion," *The Thomist* 46 (1985): 248–87; John R. Connery, "The Non-Infallible Moral Teaching of the Church," *The Thomist* 51 (1987): 1–16; William C. Spohn, "The Magisterium and Morality," *Theological Studies* 54 (1993): 95–111.

[48] The first edition of *Unfehlbar?Eine Anfrage* was published on July 18, 1970; *Pastor Aeternus* was promulgated on July 18, 1870.

faith itself is a truth that the Church has from the beginning held as having been certainly revealed in Christ's promises."[49]

Although Sullivan qualifies the doctrine expressed here only as a common opinion of theologians,[50] he does not call it into question as such. Rather, accepting that there is a secondary object of infallibility, he is more interested in discussing its precise extension and limitations. Hence he focuses most of his attention on the description of the secondary object as including 'those things, without which this deposit cannot be properly safeguarded and explained'.

Sullivan places a great deal of emphasis on the criterion of necessity. The secondary object does not include every matter of faith and morals connected with divine revelation – a view which he finds reflected in many of the pre-conciliar manuals of theology – but only those matters of faith and morals which are necessarily required for the protection or exposition of divine revelation. For Sullivan, the phrases 'connected to divine revelation' and 'necessarily required for safeguarding or expounding divine revelation' are not equivalent. The former is broader; the latter more restrictive. And it is the more restrictive formulation which appears in the First Vatican Council's unfinished schema on the Church,[51] and then again in the Theological Commission's official

---

[49] Congregation for the Doctrine of the Faith, Declaration in Defense of the Catholic Doctrine on the Church Against Certain Errors of the Present Day *Mysterium Ecclesiae* (24 Jun. 1973), § 3: "Secundum autem catholicam doctrinam, infallibilitas Magisterii Ecclesiae non solum ad fidei depositum se extendit, sed etiam ad ea, sine quibus hoc depositum rite nequit custodiri et exponi. Extensio vero illius infallibilitatis ad ipsum fidei depositum, est veritas quam Ecclesia inde ab initiis pro comperto habuit in promissionibus Christi esse revelatam" (AAS 65 [1973]: 401).

[50] Sullivan claims that the term 'according to Catholic doctrine' employed here by the CDF refers to "doctrines which are commonly held by Catholic theologians to be certain, but are not necessarily revealed truths, and are not dogmas of faith" (Sullivan, *Magisterium*, 134). He is certainly correct that it is not necessarily a revealed truth, and as such, not strictly a dogma of faith; but the implication that it belongs to the field of free theological opinion is false, as we have already seen.

[51] *Schema Primum De Ecclesia*, can. 9: "veritates quae necessario requiruntur, ut revelationis depositum integrum custodiatur" (Msi, 51:552).

explanation at Vatican II,[52] and now also in the CDF Declaration *Mysterium Ecclesiae*.[53] Sullivan thus introduces us, without spelling it out in these terms, to a tertiary object of the magisterium. He separates the generic category of faith and morals into three distinct groups: (1) divinely revealed matters of faith and morals; (2) non-revealed but necessarily required matters of faith and morals; and (3) non-required but still connected matters of faith and morals. The simpler explanation, of course, which avoids having to resort to the novelty of a tertiary object, is that these two ways of describing the secondary object of infallibility are equivalent. In fact, this equivalency appears in another explanation of the Theological Commission at Vatican II. In response to the observation of four council fathers that nothing is said in the text of *Lumen gentium* about the infallibility of the Church regarding things connected (*connexa*) with divine revelation, the Theological Commission replied that the equivalent (*aequivalenter*) is said in the lines just explained in terms of necessity.[54]

Nevertheless, by making this threefold division of the object of the magisterium, Sullivan is now in a position to consider whether in particular matters of faith or morals the Church might not be able to teach infallibly at all, and his first topic of discussion is the natural moral law, and in particular, the specific moral norms of the natural law. He begins by considering a number of arguments put forward by those who claim that the magisterium is able to speak infallibly about specific moral norms. There are indeed strong speculative arguments that can be and have been made. For example, the schema on the Church prepared for the Second Vatican Council by the Preparatory Theological Commission argued thus:

> "Since this same magisterium is the ministry of salvation by which men are taught the way they must follow in order to be able to attain to eternal life, it therefore has the office and the right of interpreting and

---

[52] AS, III/1, 251; cited above, p. 31, n. 42.

[53] CDF, *Mysterium Ecclesiae*, § 3; cited above, p. 34, n. 6.

[54] AS III/8, 89: "166 – Pag. 68, linn. 25–30: Relate ad integram suffragationem, observant 4 Patres quod in textu nihil dicitur de «infallibilitate Ecclesiae circa *connexa* cum Deposito Revelationis». R. – Dicitur aequivalenter ib. linn. 28–30."

of infallibly declaring not only the revealed law but also the natural law, and of making judgments about the objective conformity of all human actions with the teaching of the Gospel and the divine law."[55]

The only response which Sullivan makes to this line of argument is to suggest that its non-inclusion in the finally promulgated documents of Vatican II should be taken as a sign that most of the bishops disagreed with it. Even if this were true, we may be grateful that it is not the private opinions of the majority of bishops which constitutes the magisterium. As a speculative argument, it loses nothing of its force from having been discarded together with most of the texts prepared before the council.

Another argument, this time based on the positive teaching of the Church, is described as "rather simplistic" by Sullivan, although "still sometimes heard."[56] He formulates it syllogistically: "The magisterium is infallible in matters of faith and morals: but particular norms of the natural law are matters of morals; therefore the magisterium can speak infallibly about them."[57] Whether or not it is simplistic, it is certainly a simple argument, and all the more persuasive for that. But Sullivan contests the major premise, which presumes that the phrase 'matters of faith and morals', given in the First Vatican Council's definition of papal infallibility, means '*all* matters of faith and morals' rather than, as he would have it, '*divinely revealed* matters of faith and morals' or possibly also '*necessarily required* matters of faith and morals'.[58]

For support, Sullivan appeals to Bishop Gasser and his explanation of the deputation's rejection of the suggestion made to amend the phrase specifying the object of infallibility so that is should read: "in matters of faith and the principles of morals."[59]

---

[55] AS I/4, 48: "Cum vero idem magisterium sit ministerium salutis, quo homines docentur quam viam sequi debeant ut ad aeternam vitam valeant pervenire, ideo munus et ius illi competunt non modo revelatam sed et naturalem legem interpretandi et infallibiliter declarandi, et de obiectiva conformitate omnium actionum humanarum cum evangelica doctrina et divina lege iudicandi." English translation provided by Sullivan, *Magisterium*, 140–41.

[56] Sullivan, *Magisterium*, 140.

[57] Ibid.

[58] Italics added for emphasis.

[59] This suggestion was made by Bishop Colet of Lucon, France (Msi, 52:1130).

Gasser explains: "Furthermore the principles of morals are able to be other merely philosophical principles of natural moral goodness, which do not pertain to the deposit of faith in every respect."[60] From this answer Sullivan concludes that, "The term *res fidei et morum* was not understood at Vatican I to embrace all possible questions of natural morality."[61]

However, Sullivan fails to mention the first and major portion of Gasser's answer, which is that, "This expression would be completely new whereas the expression 'matter of faith and morals,' i.e. doctrine of faith and morals, is very well known and every theologian knows what is to be understood by these words."[62] In order to get a good idea of what 'every theologian' understood by those words, one need not look beyond the prominent Jesuit theologians Johann Baptist Franzelin and Joseph Kleutgen, both of whom were present at the First Vatican Council as experts and advisors. Sullivan himself notes that each one includes the whole natural law under matters of faith and morals.[63] This consensus is firmly rooted in the tradition of St Robert Bellarmine, who defends the proposition which says:

> "Not only in decrees of faith is the supreme pontiff unable to err, but neither in precepts of morals, which are prescribed for the whole Church, and which are concerned with things necessary for salvation, either those which are good in themselves, or those which are evil."[64]

---

[60] Gasser, *The Gift of Infallibility*, 69: "Insuper principia morum possunt esse alia mere philosophia naturalis honestatis, quae non sub omni respecta pertinent ad depositum fidei" (Msi, 52:1224).

[61] Sullivan, *Magisterium*, 140.

[62] Gasser, *The Gift of Infallibility*, 68–69: "vox ista . . . omnino nova . . . vox res fidei et morum, doctrina fidei sit notissima, et unusquisque theologus scit quid sub his verbis sit intelligendum" (Msi, 52:1224).

[63] Joseph Kleutgen, S.J., *Die Theologie der Vorzeit verteidigt*, 2nd ed., vol. 1 (Innsbruck: Rauch, 1878), 146; Johann Baptist Franzelin, S.J., *Tractatus de divina traditione et scriptura* (Rome: Propaganda Fide; Turin: Marietti, 1870), 110, 547–51. Cited by Sullivan, *Magisterium*, 137. O'Connor makes the same point in *The Gift of Infallibility*, 69; as does Germain Grisez, "Infallibility and Specific Moral Norms," 265–66.

[64] My translation of Bellarmine, *De summo pontifice*, lib. 4, cap. 5: "Non solum in decretis fidei errare non potest summus pontifex, sed neque in praeceptis morum, quae toti Ecclesiae praescribuntur, et quae in rebus necessariis ad salutem, vel in iis quae per se bona, vel mala sunt, versantur."

The original schema drafted by the Central Preparatory Commission for Vatican II shows that the common understanding of the phrase 'faith and morals' among theologians still included the whole natural law at least until the 1960s.[65]

It can hardly be claimed, therefore, that the phrase 'faith and morals' was not intended to be understood as including the whole natural moral law. But if this is the case, what then did Gasser mean by the second part of his answer, in which he rejected the phrase 'principles of morals' because not every principle of morals pertains in every respect to the deposit of faith? Germain Grisez suggests that the key may lie in Gasser's use of *'naturalis honestatis'* where he says, "The principles of morals are able to be other merely philosophical principles of natural moral goodness (*naturalis honestatis*), which do not pertain to the deposit of faith in every respect."[66] It is not principles of the natural moral law which are said not to pertain in every respect to the deposit of faith, but principles of natural *honestas*, which, Grisez suggests, has connotations of social convention and etiquette.[67]

In any case, one must also bear in mind what the proposed amendment was trying to accomplish and what the deputation was aiming to preserve by rejecting it. In his proposal for this amendment, Bishop Colet stated that he was seconding the suggestion of Bishop Yusto of Burgos, Spain, who wanted to exclude particular determinations of the moral law from the sphere of infallibility by limiting the object to "general principles of morals."[68] The way in which Yusto and Colet wanted the object of infallibility to be defined is therefore quite similar to the way in

---

Cardinal Manning reviews the teachings of Hervaeus Natalis (1260–1323), St Antoninus (1389–1459), Melchior Cano (1509–1560), Domingo Bañez (1528–1604), St Robert Bellarmine (1542–1621), Francisco Suárez (1548–1617), Gregory of Valentia (1550–1603), and St Alphonsus Ligouri (1696–1787), and concludes: "The phrase, then, 'faith and morals' signifies the whole revelation of faith; the whole way of salvation through faith; or the whole supernatural order, with all that is essential to the sanctification and salvation of man through Jesus Christ" (Henry Edward Manning, *The Vatican Council and Its Definitions: A Pastoral Letter to the Clergy* [London: Longmans, Green, and Co., 1870], 60).

[65] AS I/4, 48; cited above, p. 36, n. 12.
[66] Gasser, *The Gift of Infallibility*, 69; cited above, p. 38, n. 17.
[67] Grisez, "Infallibility and Specific Moral Norms," 266–67.
[68] Cited by O'Connor, *The Gift of Infallibility*, 82 (cf. Msi, 52:853).

which Sullivan understands it to have been defined, namely, as excluding specific moral norms. Hence there is more than a touch of irony in the deputation's rejection of the suggestion as being too broadly formulated.

b) CDF: Donum veritatis

In 1990 the Congregation for the Doctrine of the Faith issued the Instruction *Donum veritatis* in order to clarify the place and role of theologians within the Church and especially in relation to the magisterium.[69] In the background of this Instruction stands the figure of Charles Curran, a Catholic priest and theologian who played a leading role in the highly public dissent which greeted *Humanae vitae* in 1968,[70] and who continued thereafter to dissent loudly from the Church's teaching on contraception, abortion, euthanasia, fornication, homosexual acts, and the indissolubility of marriage, among other things.[71] The claim that the Church is not competent to speak infallibly about specific moral norms of the natural law such as these is one of Curran's central claims in defense of his dissent.[72] His dismissal from the faculty of the Catholic University of America in 1986, in response to a decision of the CDF,[73] spurred an intense discussion of the legitimacy of

---

[69] Congregation for the Doctrine of the Faith, Instruction on the Ecclesial Vocation of the Theologian *Donum veritatis* (24 May 1990).

[70] See, for example, the "Statement by Theologians," *New York Times* (31 Jul. 1968); *Contraception: Authority and Dissent*, ed. Charles E. Curran (New York: Herder and Herder, 1969); Charles E. Curran et al, *Dissent In and For the Church* (New York: Sheed and Ward, 1969); *The Responsibility of Dissent: The Church and Academic Freedom* (New York: Sheed and Ward, 1969).

[71] A list of some of Curran's dissenting positions is given by the Congregation for the Doctrine of the Faith, *Letter to Father Charles Curran* (25 Jul. 1986).

[72] See, for example, Charles E. Curran, "Authority and Dissent in the Roman Catholic Church," in *Vatican Authority and American Catholic Dissent: The Curran Case and Its Consequences*, ed. William W. May (New York: Crossroad, 1987), 29–30.

[73] Curran was dismissed after the CDF notified the University of its decision that he would no longer be considered suitable or eligible to teach Catholic theology in an ecclesiastical institution (CDF, *Letter to Father Charles Curran*, AAS 79 [1987]: 116–18).

theological dissent, and especially public dissent.[74] *Donum veritatis* represents the contribution of the CDF to this debate.[75]

Francis Sullivan offers his commentary on this Instruction in the form of a series of questions that occur to him on the basis of his reading of the text. One of his questions is: "What kind of nonrevealed truth can be the object of definitive teaching?"[76] This question arises because the document twice utilizes the 'broad' description of the secondary object as consisting of matters "intimately connected" (*intime conectuntur*) or "strictly and intimately connected" (*stricte et intime conectuntur*) with divine revelation without any reference to a criterion of necessity.[77] Sullivan is clearly perplexed by this, and openly wonders whether the CDF is intending to expand the boundaries of the object of infallibility, but he contents himself with the observation that the document nowhere explicitly claims that the Church can speak infallibly on the whole of the natural law.[78] It does, however, address the authority and competence of the magisterium in this

---

[74] See, for example, the collection of essays *Vatican Authority and American Catholic Dissent*, ed. May; Ladislas Orsy, S.J., "Magisterium: Assent and Dissent," *Theological Studies* 48 (1987): 473–97. At the time, Curran himself published a book entitled *Faithful Dissent* (Kansas City: Sheed and Ward, 1986); more recently, he penned *Loyal Dissent: Memoirs of a Catholic Theologian* (Washington, D.C.: Georgetown University Press, 2006).

[75] A collection of largely critical essays quickly appeared under the title of *Streitgespräch um Theologie und Lehramt: Die Instruktion über die kirchliche Berufung des Theologen in der Diskussion*, ed. Peter Hünermann and Dietmar Mieth (Frankfurt: Knecht, 1991). Joseph Ratzinger, the prefect at that time of the CDF, also contributed a work entitled (in English) *The Nature and Mission of Theology: Approaches to Understanding Its Role in the Light of Present Controversy*. Trans. Adrian Walker (San Francisco: Ignatius Press, 1995).

[76] Francis A. Sullivan, S.J. "The Theologian's Ecclesial Vocation and the 1990 CDF Instruction," *Theological Studies* 52 (1991): 55.

[77] CDF, *Donum veritatis*, § 16a: "Munus divinae Revelationis depositum sancte custodiendi et fideliter exponendi suapte natura secumfert Magisterium definitive proponere posse sententias quae, etiam si non continentur in veritatibus fidei, ipsis tamen intime conectuntur, adeo ut indoles definitiva talium affirmationum a Revelatione ipsa tandem derivet" (AAS 82 [1990]: 1557); CDF, *Donum veritatis*, § 23: "Cum idem proponit definitive veritates respicientes fidem et mores, quae etiam si non pertinent proprie ad Revelationem, stricte et intime ei conectuntur, ipsae firmiter amplectendae et retinendae sunt" (AAS 82 [1990]: 1559–60).

[78] Sullivan, "The Theologian's Ecclesial Vocation," 57–58.

regard. The translation utilized by Sullivan is from the English version published in *Origins*.[79] The relevant passage reads as follows:

> "What concerns morality can also be the object of the authentic Magisterium because the Gospel, being the Word of Life, inspires and guides the whole sphere of human behavior. The Magisterium, therefore, has the task of discerning, by means of judgments normative for the consciences of believers, those acts which in themselves conform to the demands of faith and foster their expression in life and those which, on the contrary, because intrinsically evil, are incompatible with such demands. By reason of the connection between the orders of creation and redemption and by reason of the necessity, in view of salvation, of knowing and observing the whole moral law, the competence of the Magisterium also extends to that which concerns the natural law."[80]

Notably missing from the authoritative Latin text, however, is the little word 'also' in the opening line. As it stands in the English translation, it might appear that something else is under consideration here other than the secondary object of definitive (infallible) teaching which was the topic of the preceding lines:

> "By its nature, the task of religiously guarding and loyally expounding the deposit of divine Revelation (in all its integrity and purity), implies that the Magisterium can make a pronouncement "in a definitive way" on propositions which, even if not contained among the truths of faith, are nonetheless intimately connected with them, in such a way, that the

---

[79] *Origins* 20.8 (5 Jul. 1990): 117–26. This is the version also present on the website of the Holy See (accessed on 7 May 2012).

[80] CDF, *Donum veritatis*, § 16b: "Ea quae ad mores pertinent, possunt materiam constituere Magisterii authentici, quia Evangelium, Verbum vitae, inspirat et moderatur totum humanarum actionum ambitum. Quare ad Magisterium spectat munus discernendi, ope iudiciorum quae conscientiam fidelium obstringant, actus qui in se ipsis fidei necessitatibus sint conformes eius que manifestationem in actione vitae promoveant, ab actis, qui e contra ex intrinseca malitia cum iisdem necessitatibus componi non possunt. Ob vinculum quod inter ordinem creationis et ordinem redemptionis intercedit, et ob necessitatem ad salutem cognoscendi et observandi universam legem moralem, competentia Magisterii ad ea etiam extenditur, quae legem naturalem respiciunt" (AAS 82 [1990]: 1557).

definitive character of such affirmations derives in the final analysis from revelation itself."[81]

If the line following this paragraph goes on to say that the magisterium can 'also' teach authoritatively about the whole natural law, then one might reasonably conclude with Sullivan that the ability to speak infallibility is not being claimed for such teaching. But if that line simply reads, as it does in the Latin text: "Those things which pertain to morals are able to constitute matter of the authoritative Magisterium, because the Gospel, the Word of life, inspires and moderates the whole ambit of human action" (*Ea quae ad mores pertinent, possunt materiam constituere Magisterii authentici, quia Evangelium, Verbum vitae, inspirat et moderatur totum humanarum actionum ambitum*), then the statement about the magisterium's competence to teach authoritatively on the whole of the natural law appears rather as an explanation of the aforementioned ability to teach definitively about non-revealed matters of morals.

At this point, we need to look more closely at the variance in formulation between *Donum veritatis*, on the one hand, and *Mysterium Ecclesiae* and *Lumen gentium*, on the other. Why is it that the secondary object of infallibility is sometimes described by the Church as consisting of matters which are 'intimately connected' with divine revelation, and at other times described as pertaining to matters which are 'required' for the protection or exposition of divine revelation? Moreover, how can all this be summed up in the single phrase 'matters of faith and morals'? One answer would be to posit some extent of disagreement between the teaching of Vatican I, Vatican II, and the CDF, respectively. Another approach is to consider 'matters of faith' and 'matters of morals' distinctly, and in relation to the ultimate aim or purpose of the Church, which is the salvation of souls for the glory of God.

It would be inadequate to say that the Church's charism of infallibility is given to her in order to preserve and expound the deposit of faith without error. The higher purpose of the gift is to lead men unerringly to salvation; and in order to be saved, it is necessary for men and women both to believe rightly (faith) and to

---

[81] CDF, *Donum veritatis*, § 16a; cited above, p. 41, n. 34.

behave rightly (morals). In order to guide men unerringly in right faith, the Church possesses the gift of infallibility with regard to 'matters of faith'; in order thus to guide men in right action, the Church is infallible in 'matters of morals' as well.

The answer to the question as to what exactly is included within the field of morals is ultimately quite simple: it is morals, moral matters, questions of good and evil, right and wrong in human actions. No one understands the word 'morals' to signify anything else. The primary object of the infallible magisterium as it pertains to morals relates to divinely revealed moral laws, and the secondary object to naturally knowable moral laws. With regard to practical, moral actions, therefore, it is sufficient to describe the secondary object of infallibility as consisting of matters which have a strict and intimate connection with divine revelation, because every human action has, as Pope Pius XI teaches, "a necessary connection with man's last end, and therefore cannot be withdrawn from the dictates of the divine law, of which the Church is guardian, interpreter and infallible mistress."[82] All moral doctrines are strictly and intimately connected to the divinely revealed law through their necessary connection to man's final end; this is true of specific moral norms above all, for man lives and acts in the realm of the concrete and particular.

With regard to matters of faith, however, it is not so immediately clear which non-revealed speculative truths are strictly and intimately connected with revealed truths. Many physical and historical truths have little or no connection to truths of divine revelation. Those which have a strict connection with the deposit of faith are those which are required in order to safeguard or expound this deposit. In fact, this requirement is precisely the basis of the connection. The fact that Julius Caesar, for example, was killed by Brutus and Cassius, has no direct bearing on the deposit of faith. The fact that Eugenio Pacelli was legitimately

---

[82] Pope Pius XI, Encyclical Letter on Christian Education *Divini illius Magistri* (31 Dec. 1929), § 18: "Idque potest Ecclesia, sive quod, ut societas est perfecta, sui iuris est in praesidiis adiumentisque deligendis sibique comparandis, quae ad FINEM conferant suum; sive quod quaelibet doctrina atque institutio, perinde ut omnis hominum actio, ex ultimo fine necessario pendet, adeoque divinae legis praeceptis non subiici nequit, cuius quidem Ecclesia est erroribus omnino immunis custos, interpres ac magistra" (AAS 22 [1930]: 54).

elected as pope by the College of Cardinals on March 2, 1939, is intimately connected with our faith in the bodily Assumption of the Blessed Virgin Mary into heaven, because this dogma was defined by him as Pope Pius XII in 1950. In matters of faith, the category of 'required for the protection or exposition of the deposit of faith' is not a stricter category than 'intimately connected with the deposit of faith'. It is rather explanatory of the latter. This explanation is introduced into some of the magisterial texts in order to clarify not so much what belongs to morals, but what belongs to faith.

c) The Catechism, Canon Law, and the Profession of Faith

There are a few more magisterial documents touching upon the secondary object of the magisterium which we may briefly review here. The new *Catechism of the Catholic Church* (1997) describes the secondary object of infallibility in one place as containing "truths having a necessary connection with"[83] divine revelation, and in another place as containing "all those elements of doctrine, including morals, without which the saving truths of the faith cannot be preserved, explained, or observed."[84] The first formulation recalls the language of *Donum veritatis*, while the second refers explicitly to *Lumen gentium* and *Mysterium*

---

[83] *Catechism of the Catholic Church* (1997), § 88: "Ecclesiae Magisterium auctoritatem a Christo receptam plene adhibet, cum dogmata definit, id est, cum, modo populum christianum ad adhaesionem fidei irrevocabilem vinculante, veritates proponit in Revelatione divina contentas, vel etiam cum veritates cum his conexionem necessariam habentes modo proponit definitivo." The Latin typical edition here leaves behind the surprising claim made in the first edition, composed in French, to the effect that definitively taught doctrines belonging to the secondary object are to be accepted as dogmas with the assent of faith: "Le Magistère de l'Eglise engage pleinement l'autorité qu'il tient du Christ quand il définit des dogmes, c'est-à-dire quand il propose, sous une forme obligeant le peuple chrétien à une adhésion irrévocable de foi, des vérités contenues dans la Révélation divine ou des vérités ayant avec celles-là un lien nécessaire" (*Catéchisme de l'Eglise catholique* [1992], § 88).

[84] *Catechism of the Catholic Church* (1997), § 2035: "Gradus supremus participationis in auctoritate Christi a charismate praestatur *infallibilitatis*. Hoc «tantum patet quantum divinae Revelationis patet depositum»; ad omnia etiam doctrinae, doctrina morali ibi inclusa, extenditur elementa, sine quibus veritates fidei salutares nequeunt custodiri, exponi vel observari."

Ecclesiae. Moreover, the generic assertion of Vatican I still finds an echo in a text which states simply: "Christ endowed the Church's shepherds with the charism of infallibility in matters of faith and morals."[85]

The authority of the magisterium to teach about specific moral norms of the natural law is also addressed, although an explicit affirmation of the Church's infallibility with regard to such is still lacking.[86] Still taking advantage of this, Sullivan repeats his appeal to Bishop Gasser in a note on the secondary object of infallibility written after the publication of the first edition of the new Catechism. Here he poses again the question, "whether it is enough for something to be a 'matter of morals' for it to be potential matter for infallible definition."[87] His answer continues along the same lines we have seen before:

> "One might be led to give an affirmative answer to this question by the way that Vatican I defined the dogma of papal infallibility. It said that the pope speaks with infallibility when he defines *doctrinam de fide vel moribus*, "doctrine of faith or morals." Without a knowledge of the *Acta* of Vatican I, one could easily take this to mean that the pope can infallibly define any moral issue whatsoever. But the official explanation of the definition of papal infallibility given by Bishop Gasser, spokesman for the *Deputatio de Fide*, shows clearly that the phrase "doctrine of faith or morals" in this context refers to doctrine that is either revealed or is required for the defense or explanation of revealed truth."[88]

The column of Gasser's speech to which he refers, however, does nothing to dissuade the attentive reader from his first

---

[85] *Catechism of the Catholic Church* (1997), § 890: "Ad hoc servitium adimplendum, Christus Pastores charismate donavit infallibilitatis in rebus fidei et morum."

[86] *Catechism of the Catholic Church* (1997), § 2036: "Magisterii auctoritas etiam ad specifica *legis naturalis* extenditur praecepta, quia eorum observantia, a Creatore postulata, necessaria est ad salutem. Ecclesiae Magisterium, in memoriam revocans legis naturalis praescripta, essentialem exercet partem sui prophetici muneris, hominibus nuntiandi quid ipsi vere sint eisque commemorandi quid ipsi coram Deo esse debeant."

[87] Francis A. Sullivan, S.J., "The 'Secondary Object' of Infallibility," *Theological Studies* 54 (1993): 544.

[88] Sullivan, "Secondary Object," 544.

comprehension of the meaning of the words 'faith and morals'. In the referenced portion of his text, Gasser says this:

> "Together with revealed truths, there are, as I said a little while ago, other truths more or less strictly connected. These truths, although they are not revealed *in se*, are nevertheless required in order to guard fully, explain properly and define efficaciously the very deposit of faith."[89]

Sullivan wants to read three categories of truths into this statement: (1) revealed truths of faith and morals; (2) non-revealed truths of faith and morals which are required in order to defend, explain, and define the deposit of faith – these would be the 'more strictly' connected; and (3) non-revealed truths of faith and morals which are not required to defend, explain, or define the deposit of faith: the 'less strictly' connected. But this cannot stand. Not only is there no real evidence for this in the portion of Gasser's text to which Sullivan refers, but we have already seen Gasser explicitly divide the whole genus of faith and morals into two (not three) categories, and attribute infallibility to the whole genus.[90]

Finally, there is the very important concluding formula of the *Professio fidei* developed by the CDF and incorporated into the universal law of the Church. The predecessor of the *Professio* in its current form was the *formula Tridentina* dating from the Council of Trent, to which Pope St Pius X had added the *Oath against Modernism* in 1910. These were supplanted by a very brief formula in 1967, which was then expanded in 1988. The 1988 version was then re-promulgated in 1998 without alteration in conjunction with Pope John Paul II's Motu Proprio *Ad tuendam fidem*, by which he caused the contents of the extended formula of the *Professio* to be inserted into the current *Code of Canon Law* and the *Code of Canons of the Eastern Churches*.[91] After the

---

[89] Gasser, *The Gift of Infallibility*, 76; cited above, p. 21, n. 17.

[90] See especially Gasser, *The Gift of Infallibility*, 81; Msi, 52:1316.

[91] Congregation for the Doctrine of the Faith, *Formula deinceps adhibenda in casibus in quibus iure praescribitur Professio Fidei loco formulae Tridentinae et iuramenti antimodernistici* (17 Jul. 1967); *Professio fidei et Iusiurandum fidelitatis in suscipiendo officio nomine Ecclesiae exercendo* (1 Jul. 1988); *Professio fidei et Iusiurandum fidelitatis in suscipiendo officio nomine Ecclesiae exercendo una cum nota doctrinali adnexa* (29 Jun. 1998); Pope John Paul II, Apostolic Letter Motu Proprio *Ad tuendam fidem* (18 May 1998).

recitation of the Niceno-Constantinopolitan Creed, the current *Professio fidei* continues with three additional paragraphs, cited here in full:

> "With firm faith, I also believe everything contained in the word of God, whether written or handed down in Tradition, which the Church, either by a solemn judgment or by the ordinary and universal Magisterium, sets forth to be believed as divinely revealed."[92]

> "I also firmly accept and hold each and everything definitively proposed by the Church regarding teaching on faith and morals."[93]

> "Moreover, I adhere with religious submission of will and intellect to the teachings which either the Roman Pontiff or the College of Bishops enunciate when they exercise their authentic Magisterium, even if they do not intend to proclaim these teachings by a definitive act."[94]

A complete outline of the magisterium can be found in these three paragraphs: the twofold subject of pope and bishops appears in the third paragraph; the reference to a universal teaching authority in the first paragraph implies a distinction from a particular power; also in the first paragraph, the proposition of the ordinary magisterium is distinguished from the solemn judgment of the extraordinary magisterium; and the distinction between the primary and secondary object of the magisterium can be seen in the difference between the first and second paragraphs. Apropos of the present discussion, the second paragraph presents the object of

---

[92] CDF, *Professio fidei* (1998): "Firma fide quoque credo ea omnia quae in verbo Dei scripto vel tradito continentur et ab Ecclesia sive sollemni iudicio sive ordinario et universali Magisterio tamquam divinitus revelata credenda proponuntur" (AAS 90 [1998]: 542). Cf. *Code of Canon Law* (1983), can. 750, § 1; *Code of Canons of the Eastern Churches* (1990), can. 598, § 1.

[93] CDF, *Professio fidei* (1998): "Firmiter etiam amplector ac retineo omnia et singula quae circa doctrinam de fide vel moribus ab eadem definitive proponuntur" (AAS 90 [1998]: 542). Cf. *Code of Canon Law* (1983), can. 750, § 2; *Code of Canons of the Eastern Churches* (1990), can. 598, § 2.

[94] CDF, *Professio fidei* (1998): "Insuper religioso voluntatis et intellectus obsequio doctrinis adhaereo quas sive Romanus Pontifex sive Collegium episcoporum enuntiant cum Magisterium authenticum exercent etsi non definitivo actu easdem proclamare intendant" (AAS 90 [1998]: 543). Cf. *Code of Canon Law* (1983), can. 752; *Code of Canons of the Eastern Churches* (1990), can. 599.

infallibility simply as 'doctrine of faith or morals' (*doctrinam de fide vel moribus*).[95]

---

[95] Umberto Betti was therefore right to include the entire moral law explicitly within the adequate object of infallibility in his commentary which appeared in *L'Osservatore Romano* on the facing page with the new *Professio fidei* in 1989: "Può rientrare nell'oggetto di definizioni irreformabili, anche se non di fede, tutto ciò che si riferisce alla legge naturale, essa pure espressione della volontà di Dio. A tale titolo appartiene anch'essa alla competenza interpretativa e propositiva della Chiesa, in ragione del suo ministero di salvezza" (Umberto Betti, O.F.M., "Considerazioni dottrinali," *L'Osservatore Romano* [25 Feb. 1989]: 6). This commentary was also published in *Notitia* 25 (1989): 321–25; the contrary is still maintained by Francis A. Sullivan, S.J., "Some Observations on the New Formula for the Profession of Faith," *Gregorianum* 70 (1989): 549–58.

PART II.
THE ORDINARY AND EXTRAORDINARY MODES OF EXERCISE OF PAPAL INFALLIBILITY

CHAPTER THREE

ORDINARY PAPAL INFALLIBILITY

Our second major question about the extension of papal infallibility pertains to the distinction between the ordinary and extraordinary modes of exercise of the magisterium in the Church's proposition of a doctrine. The explicit distinction is of relatively recent origin in theology, dating back only to the middle of the nineteenth century. Pope Pius IX first makes mention of an 'ordinary' exercise of the magisterium in his Apostolic Letter to the Archbishop of Munich *Tuas libenter*.[1] The distinction is taken up by the First Vatican Council in the Constitution *Dei Filius*, where the ordinary mode of teaching is contrasted with solemn judgments:

> "Wherefore, by divine and Catholic faith all those things are to be believed which are contained in the word of God as found in Scripture [or] Tradition, and which are proposed by the Church as matters to be believed as divinely revealed, whether by her solemn judgment or in her ordinary and universal magisterium."[2]

---

[1] Pope Pius IX, Apostolic Letter to the Archbishop of Munich *Tuas libenter* (21 Dec. 1863): "For, even if it were a matter concerning that subjection which is to be manifested by an act of divine faith, nevertheless, it would not have to be limited to those matters which have been defined by express decrees of the ecumenical Councils, or of the Roman Pontiffs and of this See, but would have to be extended also to those matters which are handed down as divinely revealed by the ordinary teaching power of the whole Church spread throughout the world, and therefore, by universal and common consent are held by Catholic theologians to belong to faith" (D 1683).

[2] Vatican I, *Dei Filius*, cap. 3: "Porro fide divina et catholica ea omnia credenda sunt, quae in verbo Dei scripto vel tradito continentur, et ab ecclesia sive solemni iudicio sive ordinario et universali magisterio tamquam divinitus revelata credenda proponuntur" (DEC, 807).

One of the fullest statements of the magisterium on the nature of the distinction between the ordinary and extraordinary modes of teaching appears in Pope Pius XI's Encyclical Letter *Mortalium animos*:

> [Ordinary:] For the teaching authority of the Church, which in the divine wisdom was constituted on earth in order that revealed doctrines might remain intact for ever, and that they might be brought with ease and security to the knowledge of men, and which is daily exercised through the Roman Pontiff and the Bishops who are in communion with him,

> [Extraordinary:] has also the office of defining, when it sees fit, any truth with solemn rites and decrees, whenever this is necessary either to oppose the errors or the attacks of heretics, or more clearly and in greater detail to stamp the minds of the faithful with the articles of sacred doctrine which have been explained. But in the use of this extraordinary teaching authority no newly invented matter is brought in, nor is anything new added to the number of those truths which are at least implicitly contained in the deposit of Revelation, divinely handed down to the Church: only those which are made clear which perhaps may still seem obscure to some, or that which some have previously called into question is declared to be of faith.[3]

In all three cases, the principal point is the same. Each statement is insisting that the same response is owed by the faithful to the

---

[3] Pope Pius XI, Encyclical Letter on Religious Unity *Mortalium animos* (6 Jan. 1928), § 9: "Etenim Ecclesiae magisterium – quod divino consilio in terris constitutum est ut revelatae doctrinae cum incolumes ad perpetuitatem consistèrent, tum ad cognitionem hominum facile tutoque traducerentur – quamquam per Romanum Pontificem et Episcopos cum eo communionem habentes cotidie exercetur, id tamen complectitur muneris, ut, si quando aut haereticorum erroribus atque oppugnationibus obsisti efficacius aut clarius subtiliusque explicata sacrae doctrinae capita in fidelium mentibus imprimi oporteat, ad aliquid tum sollemnibus ritibus decretisque definiendum opportune procedat. Quo quidem extraordinario magisterii usu nullum sane inventum inducitur nec quidquam additur novi ad earum summam veritatum, quae in deposito Revelationis, Ecclesiae divinitus tradito, saltem implicite continentur, verum aut ea declarantur quae forte adhuc obscura compluribus videri possint aut ea tenenda de fide statuuntur quae a nonnullis ante in controversiam vocabantur" (AAS 20 [1928]: 14).

dogmas of the faith, no matter whether these have been proposed in an extraordinary way by a solemn judgment or simply proposed through the ordinary teaching of the Church. Thus, negatively, the difference between the extraordinary solemn judgments and the ordinary teaching is not that one is more authoritative, more definitive, or more infallible than the other. Positively, Pius XI indicates that the distinctive property of the extraordinary definition is to introduce some new precision or formulation into the doctrine of the Church (yet without substantial addition to the deposit of faith), either to oppose errors and heresies or to impress upon the minds of the faithful more clearly, more precisely, or in greater detail, the articles of sacred doctrine.

With regard to the adequate act of infallible teaching, Vatican I declares the pope to be infallible in the act of 'defining' doctrine of faith or morals. This has most often been interpreted to refer only to his extraordinary definitions or solemn judgments, although there are authors who interpret it as inclusive of both ordinary and extraordinary definitons. For the sake of argument, however, we will begin by assuming the minimalist interpretation and defend the infallibility of the ordinary papal magisterium on speculative grounds.

Even if it is true that Vatican I does not define the infallibility of the pope in his ordinary teaching, it certainly does not positively exclude this, and the speculative arguments in support of it are quite strong. In spite of this, however, common theological opinion today denies the infallibility of the ordinary papal magisterium. For example, the third edition of the renowned *Lexicon für Theologie und Kirche*, simply asserts as a matter of fact: "An infallible ordinary magisterium of the pope does not exist."[4] This opinion, however, for all the placid assurance with which it is held and stated is not without some highly problematic implications.

---

[4] My translation of Beinert, "Unfehlbarkeit," 390: "Ein *unfehlbares* ordenl. Lehramt des Papstes existiert nicht."

a) Supreme Authority and Ordinary Infallibility

In the decades following the First Vatican Council, some theologians who interpreted the definition as referring only to the extraordinary papal magisterium began to press forward with speculation on this subject. A prominent example of such theological speculation is to be found in the massive French *Dictionnaire de théologie catholique* published over the course of the first half of the twentieth century. The entry on papal infallibility was contributed by Edmond Dublanchy, a priest of the Society of Mary.[5] It is a scholarly treatise on the subject running to eighty columns, in the midst of which the author sets out a clear and concise argument for the infallibility of the ordinary papal magisterium. He derives his two fundamental premises from the two decrees of the First Vatican Council.

Firstly, the definition of papal infallibility in the Constitution *Pastor Aeternus* states that the pope, when he "defines a doctrine . . possesses . . . that infallibility which the divine Redeemer willed his church to enjoy in defining doctrine."[6] From this text Dublanchy draws out the equality, or even identity, between the infallibility of the Church as a whole and the infallibility of the pope as supreme head of the Church on earth. Now Butler is right when he points out in his history of Vatican I that it is not strictly correct to assert "that the definition declares the Pope *ex cathedra* to possess the infallibility with which Christ endowed the Church."[7] It is only in the act of defining doctrine that the pope is expressly said to possess that same infallibility which the Church possesses in defining doctrine. Dublanchy's argument, therefore, relies on reasoning that this defined truth – namely, that the pope defining doctrine possesses the same infallibility as the Church possesses in defining doctrine – is a particular instance of a more general truth: namely, that the pope as supreme head of the universal Church possesses the same infallibility whole and entire

---

[5] Edmond Dublanchy, S.M., "Infaillibilité du Pape," in DTC, 7:1638–1717.

[6] Vatican I, *Pastor Aeternus*, cap. 4; cited above, p. 1, n. 3.

[7] Butler, *The Vatican Council*, 2:219.

which Christ willed to bestow upon his Church as a whole. This agrees with the explanation given by Gasser at the council, for when he states that the infallibility of the pope extends to the same object as that of the Church, he gives as the reason for this, that "the purpose of infallibility is the same in whichever mode it is exercised."[8]

The truth of this first premise has now been verified explicitly by the Second Vatican Council in *Lumen gentium*, where it states, speaking of definitions '*ex cathedra*', that "then the Roman pontiff is not delivering a judgment as a private person, but as the supreme teacher of the universal Church, in whom the Church's own charism of infallibility individually exists."[9] Dublanchy's reasoning is thus secure in establishing as his major premise that the pope individually possesses in its entirety the same infallibility possessed by the whole Church.

Dublanchy then draws his minor premise from the Constitution *Dei Filius*, where it reads: "by divine and Catholic faith all those things are to be believed which are contained in the word of God . . . and which are proposed by the Church . . . whether by her solemn judgment or in her ordinary and universal magisterium."[10] From this it appears that the Church is able to propose binding dogmas not only in her solemn judgments (i.e., extraordinary definitions), but also in her ordinary and universal teaching. Nothing is said explicitly about infallibility in this text, but it can be inferred that a power which is able to bind all of the faithful to make the act of divine faith must be infallible, else it would be able to lead the entire Church into heresy, and Christ's promises would fail in their effect (cf. Mt 16:18; 28:20). This point has also been explicitly confirmed by the Second Vatican Council, which clearly proposes the infallibility of the ordinary and

---

[8] Gasser, *The Gift of Infallibility*, 75; cited above, p. 20, n. 15.

[9] Vatican II, *Lumen gentium*, § 25: "Tunc enim Romanus pontifex non ut persona privata sententiam profert, sed ut universalis ecclesiae magister supremus, in quo charisma infallibilitatis ipsius ecclesiae singulariter inest, doctrinam fidei catholicae exponit vel tuetur" (DEC, 869–70).

[10] Vatican I, *Dei Filius*, cap. 3; cited above, p. 51, n. 2.

universal magisterium exercised by the college of bishops in union with the pope:

> "Although individual bishops do not enjoy the prerogative of infallibility, nevertheless, even though dispersed throughout the world, but maintaining the bond of communion among themselves and with the successor of Peter, when in teaching authentically matters concerning faith and morals they agree about a judgment as one that has to be definitively held, they infallibly proclaim the teaching of Christ. This takes place even more clearly when they are gathered together in an ecumenical council and are the teachers and judges of faith and morals for the whole Church. Their definitions must be adhered to with the obedience of faith."[11]

On the basis of this text, we can state that the bishops as a collective body are able to proclaim Christian doctrine infallibly both (1) in their extraordinary definitions, which can only occur when they are gathered in ecumenical council, and (2) in their ordinary teaching when they propose a doctrine of faith or morals 'as to be held definitively' (*tamquam definitive tenendam*). This latter can occur (2a) 'even' (*etiam*) when they are dispersed throughout the world, or (2b) 'more manifestly' (*manifestius*) when they are gathered in ecumenical council.

This last point, that ecumenical councils are infallible in their ordinary teaching when they propose a doctrine of faith or morals as to be held definitively, is missed by many authors, who thus hold, either explicitly or implicitly, that the ordinary teaching of the bishops in their state of dispersion has a greater authority than the ordinary teaching of the same bishops gathered together in

---

[11] Vatican II, *Lumen gentium*, § 25: "Licet singula praesules infallibilitatis praerogativa non polleant, quando tamen, etiam per orbem dispersi, sed communionis nexum inter se et cum successore Petri servantes, authentice res fidei et morum docentes in unam sententiam tamquam definitive tenendam conveniunt, doctrinam Christi infallibiliter enuntiant. Quod adhuc manifestius habetur quando, in concilio oecumenico coadunati, pro universa Ecclesia fidei et morum doctores et iudices sunt, quorum definitionibus fidei obsequio est adhaerendum" (DEC, 869).

ecumenical council.[12] Such a disparity would be inexplicable, however, since the present geographical location of the bishops can have no possible bearing on the nature and extent of their authority. This misunderstanding likely arises at least in part from the fact that ecumenical councils are always extraordinary in comparison to the state of dispersion as regards the condition of the teaching subject. It would thus be easy to equate the extraordinary situation with extraordinary teaching and the ordinary situation with ordinary teaching.

To return to Dublanchy, however, his argument can be summarized in the following syllogism: (1) the pope possesses the same infallibility as the Church (implied in *Pastor Aeternus*, confirmed by *Lumen gentium*); (2) the Church is able to teach infallibly by her ordinary magisterium (implied in *Dei Filius*, confirmed by *Lumen gentium*); (3) therefore, the pope is able to teach infallibly by his ordinary magisterium.[13]

Another prominent theologian of the inter-conciliar period was Joachim Salaverri, a Jesuit priest and author of the treatise *De Ecclesia Christi* in *Sacrae theologiae summa*, the great manual of dogmatic theology published by the Jesuit professors of Spain. The fifth edition of this famous work was printed in 1962, the same year in which the Second Vatican Council was first convened.

---

[12] The common notion that Vatican II taught nothing infallibly is based almost entirely on this misconception. See the discussion of various opinions in Francis A. Sullivan, S.J., *Creative Fidelity: Weighing and Interpreting Documents of the Magisterium* (Eugene, Or.: Wipf and Stock, 2003), 162–74; Sullivan does not take a clear position himself, but appears to favor the 'moderate' position which views the documents of Vatican II as uniformly authoritative, but non-infallible. It is true that Vatican II deliberately avoided making any extraordinary definitions, but at least the two dogmatic constitutions *Lumen gentium* and *Dei Verbum* are quite full of infallible ordinary teaching.

[13] Dublanchy sums up his argument in a single succinct sentence: "Puisque, selon le décret du concile du Vatican, le pape possède l'infaillibilité donnée par Jésus á son Église et que, pour l'Église, cette infaillibilité peut s'étendre aux actes du magistère ordinaire, dans la mesure et aux conditions précédemment indiquées, voir ÉGLISE, t. IV, col. 2193 sq., on doit affirmer que le pape enseignant seul, en vertu de son magistère ordinaire, est infaillible dans la même mesure et aux mêmes conditions" (Dublanchy, "Infaillibilité," 1705).

Within his treatment of the magisterium, Salaverri poses the question: "Is there a single or a double mode in which the Pope may exercise infallibility?"[14] Like Dublanchy, he answers in the affirmative, and his first argument parallels Dublanchy's. From the same text of *Dei Filius* he infers a double mode of infallibility (ordinary and extraordinary) which can be exercised by the teaching Church.[15] And from the same text of *Pastor Aeternus* he argues that the fathers of the First Vatican Council "suppose the general principle against the general error held by the Gallicans, which they intend to condemn, 'That the Pope is inferior to the Church also in questions of faith'."[16] He concludes:

> "Therefore, according to the Vatican, the Pope is in no way inferior to the Church in the power of teaching. But the Church has been equipped with an infallibility which she exercises in extraordinary and ordinary modes (D 1792). Therefore it is to be conceded that the Roman Pontiff exercises his infallibility in the same modes (cf. Msi, 52:1193)."[17]

[14] My translation of Joachim Salaverri, S.J., *Tractatus de Ecclesia Christi*, in *Theologia fundamentalis*, vol. 1 of *Sacrae theologiae summa*, 5th ed. (Madrid: Biblioteca de Autores Cristianos, 1962), p. 700, no. 645, Scholion 2: "Estne unus an duplex modus quo Papa infallibilitatem exercet?"

[15] Ibid.: "Ex hac Vaticani definitione infertur, Ecclesiam docentem seu Collegium Episcoporum sub Papa constitutum, *duplici modo* infallibilitatem exercere posse, *alio extraordinario* et *alio ordinario*: *mode extraordinario*, quando in Oecumenico Concilio aliquid *sollemni iudicio* definit; *modo ordinario*, quando dispersi per orbem Episcopi aliquam doctrinam ut omnino tenendam omnibus fidelibus proponunt."

[16] Ibid., pp. 700–701, no. 647: "Quaeritur ergo ulterius, utrum Summus Pontifex suam infallibilitatem exerceat etiam *modo ordinario* necne? Huic quaestioni nobis videtur respondendum 2.° *affirmative*. Nam iuxta Conc. Vaticanum, Romanus Pontifex «ea infallibilitate pollet qua Divinus Redemptor Ecclesiam suam instructam esse voluit»: D 1839, qua sententia Patres supponunt *principium generale* contra generalem, quem damnare intendunt, errorem *Gallicanorum* tenentium, «Papam esse inferiorem Ecclesia in fidei quoque quaestionibus»: cf. Msi 49,673; 52,1230."

[17] Salaverri, *Tractatus de Ecclesia Christi*, p. 701, no. 647: "Ergo, iuxta Vaticanum, Papa nullo modo est inferior Ecclesia in potestate docendi. Atqui Ecclesia instructa est infallibilitate quam exercet modis extraordinario et ordinario: D 1792. Ergo iisdem modis Romano Pontifici concedendum est suam infallibilitatem exercere (cf. Msi 52,1193)."

Salaverri also introduces a second argument for the infallibility of the ordinary papal magisterium. "In addition," he writes, citing one of the dogmatic canons of *Pastor Aeternus*, "the Supreme Pontiff has in the Church 'the total plenitude of supreme power'."[18] Since infallible teaching authority is a power which is included in the power of jurisdiction,[19] it follows that the pope must be able to exercise the charism of infallibility in every mode in which it can be exercised in the Church; and since it can be exercised in the Church both in an extraordinary and an ordinary mode, then the pope must be able to exercise it in each of these modes. "For otherwise it would have to be concluded," writes Salaverri, "that the supreme power of infallibility, at least in the mode in which it is exercised, would be more restricted in the Roman Pontiff than in the Church."[20] Since this cannot be admitted, it follows that the pope is able to speak infallibly in both the extraordinary and ordinary modes. This argument is similar to the first, but

---

[18]Ibid.: "Insuper, Summus Pontifex habet in Ecclesia «totam plenitudinem supremae potestatis»: D 1831." Cf. Vatican I, *Pastor Aeternus*, cap. 3: "So then, if anyone says that the Roman pontiff has merely an office of supervision and guidance, and not the full and supreme power of jurisdiction over the whole Church . . . or that he has only the principal part, but not the absolute fulness, of this supreme power (*totam plenitudinem huius supremae potestatis*); or that this power of his is not ordinary and immediate both over all and each of the churches and over all and each of the pastors and faithful: let him be anathema" (DEC, 814–15).

[19] This is made clear by Vatican I, *Pastor Aeternus*, cap. 4: "That apostolic primacy which the Roman pontiff possesses as successor of Peter, the prince of the apostles, includes also the supreme power of teaching" (DEC, 815). This primacy was previously defined as a "primacy of jurisdiction" (Vatican I, *Pastor Aeternus*, cap. 1). Cf. Joseph C. Fenton, "*Magisterium* and Jurisdiction in the Catholic Church," *American Ecclesiastical Review* 130 (1954): 194–201.

[20] Salaverri, *Tractatus de Ecclesia Christi*, p. 701, no. 647: "Ergo, illam habere debet *omni modo* quo suprema potestas detur in Ecclesia. Atqui suprema potestas infallibilitatis datur in Ecclesia duplici modo, *extraordinario* nempe et *ordinario*. Ergo Summus Pontifex habet potestatem infallibilitatis modo etiam *ordinario*. Secus enim concludendum esset, supremam potestatem infallibilitatis, saltem in modo quo exercetur, esse in Romano Pontifice magis restrictam quam in Ecclesia; quod sane admitti nequit, cum Summus Pontifex in Ecclesia habeat sine ulla limitatione «totam plenitudinem supremae potestatis»: D 1831."

establishes its major premise from the pope's 'total plenitude of supreme power', which is explicitly and dogmatically affirmed in the third chapter of *Pastor Aeternus*, rather than from the equality between papal and episcopal infallibility which is merely implied, albeit quite strongly, in chapter four.

b) Objections and Contrary Arguments

The opinion contrary to the thesis defended by Dublanchy and Salaverri, among others,[21] can only accurately be called semi-Gallicanism, for it admits the equality of the jurisdictional teaching power of the pope and of the episcopal college with respect to solemn judgments or definitions – which Gallicanism denied; yet it still denies the equality of papal and episcopal magisterium with respect to ordinary teaching power. Hence the magisterial power, and hence also the ecclesiastical jurisdiction of which that power is a part, would be greater in the college of bishops than in the pope. This is essentially a form of Gallicanism, even if the pope's jurisdictional inferiority to the bishops is less pronounced than in former times.[22]

Nevertheless, despite the strong arguments in favor of admitting an infallible ordinary papal magisterium, common theological opinion today denies it. We have already seen the

---

[21] Some of the most prominent proponents of ordinary papal infallibility are Joseph C. Fenton, "The Doctrinal Authority of Papal Encyclicals," *American Ecclesiastical Review* 121 (1949): 136–50, 210–20; "Infallibility in the Encyclicals," *American Ecclesiastical Review* 128 (1953): 177–98; Louis Billot, S.J., *Tractatus de Ecclesia Christi, sive continuatio theologiae de Verbo Incarnato*, 3rd ed., vol. 1 (Prati: Giachetti, 1909), 641; J.-M. Alfred Vacant, *Le magistère ordinaire de l'Eglise et ses organes* (Paris; Lyons: Delhomme et Briquet, 1887); Adolphe Tanquerey, P.S.S., *Sysnopsis theologiae dogmaticae fundamentalis*, 24th ed. (Paris: Desclée, 1937), 633f.; Joseph De Guibert, S.J., *De Christi Ecclesia*, 2nd ed. (Rome: Gregorian University Press, 1928), 260ff.

[22] Since the opponents of the Gallicans were labeled 'ultramontanists' because they followed the theological doctrine of Rome, which was 'over the mountains' from the point of view of the French, it will be amusing to see if opponents of semi-Gallicanism come to be known as 'ultra-ultramontanists'.

categorical statement of Wolfgang Beinert in the *Lexicon für Theologie und Kirche*: "An infallible ordinary magisterium of the pope does not exist."[23] Another example can be found in Richard Gaillardetz, who explicitly supports the 'dissymmetry' which I have referred to as semi-Gallicanism, claiming that it was the deliberate intention of both Vatican councils to uphold and preserve this 'dissymmetry' by distinguishing two modes (papal and episcopal) of exercising the extraordinary magisterium, but only one mode (episcopal) of exercising the ordinary magisterium.[24] He points to the meaning of the word 'universal' as it was intended to be understood in the phrase 'ordinary and universal magisterium' at Vatican I, and then wonders how it is that, "In spite of this, one still finds theological treatments that propose an infallible exercise of the pope's ordinary magisterium."[25] Gaillardetz is also afraid that emphasis on papal confirmation of the teaching of the ordinary and universal magisterium of the bishops, such as is found in the Encyclical Letter *Evangelium vitae* (1995) of Pope John Paul II, "risks creating an unintended symmetry in which this exercise of the ordinary papal magisterium is transformed into a second, papal mode of exercising the ordinary universal magisterium."[26] What is remarkable here is that Gaillardetz regards the 'dissymmetry' inherent in his own position, according to which the ordinary teaching of the collective body of bishops is infallible whereas that of the pope is not, as something positively desirable, and an affirmation of 'symmetry' or equality between the teaching power of the pope on the one hand, and the body of bishops on the other, as a danger against which to be on one's guard.

---

[23] Beinert, "Unfehlbarkeit," 390; cited above, p. 53, n. 4.

[24] Richard R. Gaillardetz, "The Ordinary Universal Magisterium: Unresolved Questions," *Theological Studies* 63 (2002): 470. The terminology is adopted from Bernard Sesboüé, "Magistère 'ordinaire' et magistère authentique," *Recherches de science religieuse* 84 (1996): 271.

[25] Gaillardetz, "The Ordinary Universal Magisterium," p. 470, n. 69.

[26] Ibid., 470.

The arguments against the infallibility of the ordinary papal magisterium are not very often made explicitly. Nevertheless, four main types can be distinguished: there are popular, speculative, positive, and historical arguments. Perhaps the most common is the popular argument which is merely an appeal to the common opinion of theologians. Joseph Komonchak, for example, in an influential essay on the ordinary papal magisterium in the context of the controversy surrounding *Humanae vitae*, simply opens with the statement, "The ordinary teaching office of the pope is commonly regarded by theologians as being non-infallible."[27] The only actual argument which Komonchak eventually references is one made by Sullivan in his early manual on ecclesiology:

> "It seems to be possible that a pope, teaching *modo ordinario*, might propose a judgment that would have to be corrected afterwards, without the whole Church being drawn into error thereby. In such a case, the divine assistance would be enough to assure that the error would be corrected before it was generally accepted by the Church and to prevent the erroneous teaching from becoming the traditional teaching of the Holy See."[28]

Although Komonchak cites this as an argument "against the claim of infallibility for the ordinary magisterium of the pope,"[29] it is in fact nothing of the kind. Rather, it is an argument against the necessity of concluding to the infallibility of the ordinary papal magisterium from considerations of the dangers of erroneous ordinary papal teaching. In other words, the argument is able to conclude that God could have chosen another way of protecting his Church from error, other than by granting infallibility to the ordinary papal magisterium; but it says nothing about whether God

---

[27] Joseph A. Komonchak, "Ordinary Papal Magisterium and Religious Assent," in *Contraception: Authority and Dissent*, ed. Charles E. Curran (New York: Herder and Herder, 1969), 106.

[28] Francis A. Sullivan, S.J., *Quaestiones theologiae fundamentalis*, vol. 1 of *De Ecclesia* (Rome: Gregorian University Press, 1963), 350. Citation taken from Komonchak, "Ordinary Papal Magisterium," 110.

[29] Komonchak, "Ordinary Papal Magisterium," 110.

has actually done so. The speculative argument which addresses the heart of the question is rather that implied by Gaillardetz in the texts cited above. This argument simply inverts the one made by Dublanchy, Salaverri, and others, by reasoning from a premised inequality of teaching power between pope and bishops to the fallibility of the ordinary papal magisterium.

There are two kinds of positive arguments, the more common of which is the argument from silence. Sullivan furnishes an example of this when he writes:

> "Vacant, Fenton, and Salaverri were Catholic theologians who taught that popes could teach with infallibility not only in solemn definitions *ex cathedra* but also in the ordinary magisterium that they exercised in such documents as papal encyclicals. Their opinion was strongly and energetically refuted by a number of other Catholic theologians, and the resulting consensus was confirmed by Vatican II, which clearly distinguished between the pope's ordinary magisterium and his exercise of the "charism of infallibility."[30]

Note here that these 'other Catholic theologians' are not named, nor are their 'strong' and 'energetic' arguments so much as outlined. Above all, note the appeal to Vatican II, which is essentially an argument from silence. The text of *Lumen gentium* does distinguish between ordinary and extraordinary papal teaching; and it only positively ascribes infallibility to the latter; but it does not positively deny it to the former, as it denies the infallibility of other individual bishops.[31] The basic reasoning inherent in Sullivan's position seems to be that the fathers of the Second Vatican Council, by not proposing the infallibility of the ordinary papal magisterium when they had to opportunity to do so, indicate that they do not accept the truth of the thesis in question. Once again, however, even if such silence could be taken as

---

[30] Francis A. Sullivan, S.J., "The Meaning of Conciliar Dogmas," in *The Convergence of Theology: A Festschrift Honoring Gerald O'Collins, S.J.*, ed. Daniel Kendall, S.J. and Stephen T. Davis (Mahwah, N.J.: Paulist Press, 2001), 80.
[31] Vatican II, *Lumen gentium*, § 25: "Although individiual bishops do not enjoy the prerogative of infallibility . . . ." (DEC, 869).

evidence of the bishops' opinions, these do not the magisterium make.

The second kind of positive argument is stronger in that it tries to find actual magisterial teaching which would appear to deny the infallibility of the ordinary papal magisterium. There is, in the words of Monsignor Fenton, a prominent professor of theology at the Catholic University of America during the decades prior to Vatican II, "one very serious argument that has been alleged against the possibility of infallible teaching within the Holy Father's ordinary *magisterium*."[32] This argument is based upon a paragraph of Pope Pius XII's Encyclical Letter *Humani generis*, which reads:

> "Nor must it be thought that what is expounded in Encyclical Letters does not of itself demand consent, since in writing such Letters the Popes do not exercise the supreme power of their Teaching Authority. For these matters are [also] taught with the ordinary teaching authority, of which it is true to say: "He who heareth you, heareth me"; and generally what is expounded and inculcated in Encyclical Letters already for other reasons appertains to Catholic doctrine. But if the Supreme Pontiffs in their official documents purposely pass judgment on a matter up to that time under dispute, it is obvious that that matter, according to the mind and will of the Pontiffs, cannot be any longer considered a question open to discussion among theologians."[33]

Fenton refers to an essay of Edmond Benard which interprets the first half of this text to mean that, although the ordinary papal

---

[32] Fenton, "Infallibility in the Encyclicals," 182.

[33] Pope Pius XII, Encyclical Letter concerning Some False Opinions Threatening to Undermine the Foundations of Catholic Doctrine *Humani generis* (12 Aug. 1950), § 20: "Neque putandum est, ea quae in Encyclicis Litteris proponuntur, assensum per se non postulare, cum in iis Pontifices supremam sui Magisterii potestatem non exerceant. Magisterio enim ordinario haec docentur, de quo illud etiam valet: «Qui vos audit, me audit»; ac plerumque quae in Encyclicis Litteris proponuntur et inculcantur, iam aliunde ad doctrinam catholicam pertinent. Quodsi Summi Pontifices in actis suis dé re hactenus controversa data opera sententiam ferunt, omnibus patet rem illam, secundum mentem ac voluntatem eorumdem Pontificum, quaestionem liberae inter theologos disceptationis iam haberi non posse" (AAS 42 [1950]: 568).

magisterium is not the supreme magisterium of the pope – which is thus equated with his extraordinary magisterium – it is still authoritative, and hence the words of Christ are applicable to both; but since infallibility is understood to be an attribute only of supreme teaching authority, it seems that the ordinary papal magisterium is not infallible. Fenton points out, however, that this interpretation rests fundamentally on an unverifiable presupposition, namely, that the phrase 'since in writing such Letters the Popes do not exercise the supreme power of their Teaching Authority' is actually expressive of papal teaching, whereas it could just as easily be read as part of the opinion being condemned. It is thus impossible to conclude with certitude from this text that the ordinary exercise of the papal magisterium is not an exercise of the supreme magisterium. And in fact, that opposite conclusion was stated by Pope John II in one of his catechetical general audiences: in his ordinary teaching the pope does exercise the supreme magisterium.[34]

The last type of argument to be leveled against the infallibility of the ordinary papal magisterium is historical in character: namely, the citation of historical examples of apparently erroneous teaching in documents of the ordinary papal magisterium. Such objections must be taken seriously and treated of carefully, on an individual basis, as the occasion arises. The most pressing difficulty, however, is surely the question of religious liberty. Just as various teachings of Popes Liberius, Vigilius, and Honorius have had to be defended in the past, so now

---

[34] Pope John Paul II, *General Audience* (10 Mar. 1993): "However, the essential task of the papal Magisterium is to explain the doctrine of the faith, and to promote knowledge of the mystery of God and the work of salvation, bringing out all the aspects of the divine plan as it unfolds in human history under the action of the Holy Spirit. This is the service to the truth that has been primarily entrusted to Peter's Successor, who in the ordinary exercise of his Magisterium is already acting not as a private person (*che già nell'esercizio ordinario del suo magistero agisce non come persona privata*), but as the supreme teacher of the universal Church (*ma come supremo maestro della Chiesa universale*), according to the precise statement of Vatican II regarding definitions ex cathedra (cf. LG 25)."

the social doctrine of Popes Pius IX and Leo XIII, among others. If it is true that the ordinary and universal teaching definitively proposed by these pontiffs on the subject of religious liberty has been contradicted and overruled by the Second Vatican Council in its Declaration *Dignitatis humanae*, as may appear to be the case from a *prima facie* reading of the texts, then this would be a serious objection indeed to the infallibility of the ordinary papal magisterium. Fortunately, however, a truly convincing reconciliation of *Dignitatis humanae* with the tradition of the papal magisterium – one which allows the teaching of both to be fully upheld, and which does not attempt to escape the problem by appealing to a 'development' of doctrine which is really an alteration – has finally been proposed by Thomas Pink of King's College, London.[35]

c) Identifying Infallible Ordinary Teaching

If it is true that the pope is able to speak infallibly not only in his extraordinary definitions, which are generally recognizable by their solemn formulae and their invocations of supreme authority, but also in his ordinary teaching, it is of the utmost importance to be able to identify accurately what of the pope's ordinary teaching is infallible and what is merely authoritative.

The first characteristic of the infallible ordinary magisterium of the pope is that it should be universal. That is, ordinary infallible papal teaching should be an act of the pope in his capacity as supreme head of the universal Church addressed to the universal Church.[36] We may thus speak of an ordinary and universal magisterium of the pope analogous to the much more

---

[35] Thomas Pink, "What Is the Catholic Doctrine of Religious Liberty?" Paper read at the Februrary 2010 Aquinas Seminar, Blackfriars, Oxford.

[36] The universal magisterium which the pope exercises as head of the universal Church is contrasted with the particular magisterium which he exercises as local bishop of the Church of the city of Rome. The infallibility of the particular magisterium of the pope is not necessarily excluded, but to defend it would require additional argumentation.

frequently discussed ordinary and universal magisterium of the bishops. It was only the latter which was implicitly declared infallible at Vatican I in the text of *Dei Filius*, where it requires that divine and Catholic faith should be given to all dogmas, whether proposed by a solemn judgment or by the Church's ordinary and universal magisterium.[37] The meaning of the word 'universal', as it is intended to be understood here, was explained by Bishop Konrad Martin of Paderborn, speaking on behalf of the deputation *de fide*, as referring specifically to the body of bishops dispersed throughout the world, and not to the magisterium exercised by the pope even as head of the universal Church.[38]

The deputation understandably did not want to settle prematurely the question of papal infallibility, which would be reserved for the following session of the council. Positively, therefore, it would be impossible to maintain that the infallibility of the ordinary and universal magisterium of the pope is directly implied in this text. Speculatively, however, we may reasonably apply the same phrase to the magisterium which the pope ordinarily exercises as head of the universal Church, and conclude that his ordinary and universal magisterium is just as infallible as that of the bishops. Although the word 'universal', as employed in the text of *Dei Filius*, is intended to signify a geographic universality, this kind of universality is relevant only a sign or an indication of a universal authority, namely, an authority which is universal in its extension to all the pastors and faithful of the whole Church. Infallibility follows upon the power of a teacher to bind the whole body of the faithful to assent to a truth of faith or morals.

---

[37] Vatican I, *Dei Filius*, cap. 3 cited above, p. 51, n. 2.

[38] Cited by Salaverri, *Tractatus de Ecclesia Christi*, p. 669, no. 552: "Eiusdem definitionis sensum ulterius determinavit Episcopus Martin, nomine eiusdem Deputationis fidei, dicens «Ratio quare vox *universali* apponitur, haec est, ut scilicet ne quis putet nos loqui hoc loco de Magisterio infallibili S.Sedis Apostolicae. Nam nullatenus ea fuit intentio Deputationis, quaestionem de infallibilitate Summi Pontificis sive directe sive indirecte tangere. Hoc igitur verbum «universali» idem fere significat, quod Sanctissimus Pater in suis Litteris Apostolicis expressit, nempe Magisterium totius Ecclesiae per orbem disperse»."

Hence, it is the universal reach of the teaching body's authority rather than the universal dispersion of that body which immediately implies infallibility. It is because the bishops dispersed throughout the world have a universal authority over the Church that their ordinary teaching is infallible. Yet popes and ecumenical councils are able to exercise universal authority over the Church as well. Granting that *Dei Filius* only positively implies the infallibility of the ordinary teaching of the bishops in their ordinary state (dispersed throughout the world), it still must be acknowledged that *Lumen gentium* extends infallibility to the ordinary teaching of the bishops in their extraordinary state (gathered in ecumenical council); and if it is legitimate to extend the meaning of the phrase 'ordinary and universal magisterium' to the ordinary teaching of ecumenical ('universal') councils, in which case the word 'universal' clearly signifies universal authority rather than universal dispersion, then it is perfectly legitimate to extend it similarly, and for the same reason, to include the ordinary teaching of the pope when he acts as universal pastor and teacher of the Church. Even though the pope is a singular subject, he exercises a magisterium which is universal in the relevant sense.[39]

Limiting our consideration, therefore, to doctrines taught by the pope acting as supreme head of the universal Church, such as is clearly the case, for example, in his encyclical letters addressed to the whole Church, what further indications must be sought in order to identify infallible ordinary papal teaching? Salaverri's solution is that the ordinary teaching of the pope is

---

[39] Cf. the reference to a 'universal' papal magisterium by Pope Pius XII, Encyclical Letter on Communism and the Church in China *Ad apostolorum principis* (29 Jun. 1958), § 7: "We openly declared that Catholics yielded to none (nor could they do so) in their true loyalty and love of their native country. Seeing also that there was being spread among you the doctrine of the so-called 'three autonomies,' We warned – by virtue of that universal teaching authority (*universali magisterio*) which We exercise by divine command – that this same doctrine as understood by its authors, whether in theory or in its consequences, cannot receive the approval of a Catholic, since it turns minds away from the essential unity of the Church."

infallible "when in things of faith or morals he proposes by his ordinary and universal magisterium a doctrine as to be believed or entirely to be held."[40] The object, of course, remains things of faith and morals; the act is ordinary in its formulation and universal in the scope of its authority; the distinguishing characteristic of infallible ordinary teaching as opposed to non-infallible ordinary teaching must therefore be the proposition of a doctrine as to be believed (*credendam*) or entirely to be held (*omnino tenendam*). In other words, one can recognize whether or not a doctrine taught by the ordinary and universal magisterium, whether of the pope or of the bishops, is taught infallibly, principally by looking at the note or theological qualification which is assigned to that doctrine, whether implicitly or explicitly. Here we need to recall the grades of theological certainty touched upon above, and the interplay between divine revelation and ecclesiastical proposition. A doctrine of faith or morals may be proposed by the Church (1) as a truth revealed by God and thus to be held by divine and Catholic faith (*de fide divina et catholica credenda*), or (2) as a theologically certain truth of Catholic doctrine, which is at least intrinsically connected with divine revelation and thus to be held definitively (*de fide definitive tenenda*), or (3) as a more or less probable theological opinion, which is to be accepted with a religious submission of will and intellect (*religioso voluntatis et intellectus obsequio adhaerendam*).

Thus, when the pope addresses himself to the universal Church and sets forth a doctrine of faith or morals as divinely revealed or as theologically certain, even without solemn formulae or invocations of supreme authority, it is to be understood that he speaks infallibly. The same is true when he censures a proposition as heretical or erroneous. Infallibility is not to be looked for, however, when a teaching is proposed in an essentially opinionative manner, such as is found most clearly in the

---

[40] Salaverri, *Tractatus de Ecclesia Christi*, p. 701, no. 648: "*Hunc autem modum ordinarium* infallibiliter docendi Romanus Pontifex adhibet, quando in rebus fidei vel morum suo ordinario et universali Magisterio doctrinam tamquam credendam vel omnino tenendam proponit."

condemnation of propositions with such censures as temerarious (*temeraria*), offensive to pious ears (*piarum aurium offensiva*), badly sounding (*male sonans*), captious (*captiosa*), scandalous (*scandalosa*), etc. Censures less than heresy and error are essentially expressive of opinions, which the faithful are therefore obliged to hold precisely as opinions. This means to hold them as morally or practically certain, or as most probably true saving the future judgment of the Church.

Positive evidence that the theological note with which a doctrine is proposed is indeed the decisive factor in identifying infallible ordinary teaching and distinguishing it from merely authoritative (non-infallible) ordinary teaching can be found in *Dei Filius* and *Lumen gentium*. The text of *Dei Filius* which is understood to imply the infallibility of the ordinary magisterium of the bishops states that doctrines which are proposed by the ordinary and universal magisterium "as to be believed as divinely revealed (*tamquam divinitus revelata credenda*) are to be believed with divine and Catholic faith (*fide divina et catholica credenda sunt*)."[41] If the Church proposes a doctrine as divinely revealed, then the faithful are bound to accept it exactly as such. Similarly, *Lumen gentium* explicitly ascribes infallibility to doctrines proposed by the ordinary magisterium of the bishops "as definitively to be held (*tamquam definitive tenendam*)."[42] Once again, if the Church proposes a doctrine as definitively to be held, which in this context means to propose it as at least theologically certain in connection with divine revelation, then it is to be accepted exactly as such. Since the same must be said of the pope singly as of the bishops collectively, then the ordinary and

---

[41] Vatican I, *Dei Filius*, cap. 3; cited above, p. 51, n. 2.

[42] Vatican II, *Lumen gentium*, § 25: "Licet singula praesules infallibilitatis praerogativa non polleant, quando tamen, etiam per orbem dispersi, sed communionis nexum inter se et cum successore Petri servantes, authentice res fidei et morum docentes in unam sententiam tamquam definitive tenendam conveniunt, doctrinam Christi infallibiliter enuntiant. Quod adhuc manifestius habetur quando, in concilio oecumenico coadunati, pro universa Ecclesia fidei et morum doctores et iudices sunt, quorum definitionibus fidei obsequio est adhaerendum" (DEC, 869).

universal magisterium of the pope is infallible when he proposes a doctrine of faith or morals as divinely revealed or definitively to be held. And if the ordinary magisterium of the pope is infallible when he proposes a doctrine either as divinely revealed (and so to be believed by faith) or as at least theologically certain (and so to be held definitively), then it also follows that the merely authoritative teaching of the ordinary papal magisterium is precisely that body of teaching which is proposed in an essentially opinionative manner as safe, probable, etc., and which is to be adhered to with a religious submission of will and intellect falling short of definitive assent.[43]

An important point to note in this connection is that it may not be enough to identify infallible ordinary teaching if a doctrine is simply set forth as true, for it is a common mode of expressing an opinion to assert that something is true even while recognizing that the opposite might be true instead. The doctrinal commentary of the CDF seems to recognize this when it says, referring to the third paragraph of the concluding formula of the *Professio fidei*: "To this paragraph belong *all those teachings – on faith and morals – presented as true or at least as sure, even if they have not been defined with a solemn judgement or proposed as definitive by the ordinary and universal Magisterium*."[44] In order to identify infallible ordinary teaching, therefore, it must be made manifest in

---

[43] *Code of Canon Law* (1983), can. 752: "Although not an assent of faith, a religious submission of the intellect and will must be given to a doctrine which the Supreme Pontiff or the college of bishops declares concerning faith or morals when they exercise the authentic magisterium, even if they do not intend to proclaim it by definitive act; therefore, the Christian faithful are to take care to avoid those things which do not agree with it." CDF, *Professio fidei* (1998): "Moreover, I adhere with religious submission of will and intellect to the teachings which either the Roman Pontiff or the College of Bishops enunciate when they exercise their authentic Magisterium, even if they do not intend to proclaim these teachings by a definitive act."

[44] CDF, *Doctrinal Commentary*, § 10: "Ad hoc comma pertinet *omnis institutio de fide et de re morali tamquam vera aut saltem tamquam certa exhibita, licet iudicio sollemni non definita nec a Magisterio ordinario et universali tamquam definita proposita*" (AAS 90 [1998]: 548).

some way that a doctrine of faith or morals is being proposed as certainly and definitely true, either as divinely revealed or as at least intimately connected with divine revelation.

In other words, the note with which the pope intends to qualify the doctrine must be discerned. If the doctrine is qualified as divinely revealed or theologically certain, then he speaks infallibly; whereas he does not if it is qualified as more or less probably true. *Lumen gentium* proposes three principal means whereby one may discern the theological note with which the pope intends to qualify a doctrine: (1) the nature of the documents; (2) the frequency of the proposition; and (3) the manner of speaking.[45] Thus, for example, the fact that a doctrine is proposed in a document such as an apostolic constitution is already strong evidence in favor of the definitive character of the teaching.

It is important to note also that, in order to identify the definitive character of ordinary papal teaching, it is sufficient that the intention of the pope to teach a doctrine as definitively to be held is made manifest in one of the ways mentioned. *Lumen gentium* says that the mind and will of the pope are made manifest 'either' (*sive*) by the nature of the documents, 'or' (*sive*) by the frequent proposition of the same doctrine, 'or' (*sive*) by the manner of expression. This runs counter to the interpretation of Dom Paul Nau, another defender of ordinary papal infallibility from the inter-conciliar period. Nau defended the infallibility of the ordinary and universal papal magisterium, but he understood it exclusively as a diachronical analogue to the synchronic universality of the bishops' ordinary infallibility. That is, just as the ordinary teaching of any one bishop is fallible, and yet the ordinary teaching of all

---

[45] Vatican II, *Lumen gentium*, § 25: "Hoc vero religiosum voluntatis et intellectus obsequium singulari ratione praestandum est Romani pontificis authentico magisterio etiam cum non ex cathedra loquitur; ita nempe ut magisterium euis supremum reverenter agnoscatur, et sententiis ab eo prolatis sincere adhaereatur, iuxta mentem et voluntatem manifestatam ipsius, quae se prodit praecipue sive indole documentorum, sive ex frequenti propositione euisdem doctrinae, sive ex dicendi ratione" (DEC, 869). Cf. CDF, *Donum veritatis*, § 24.

the bishops dispersed throughout the world is infallible, so Nau would have it that the ordinary teaching of any single pope is in itself fallible, while only the common teaching of the whole succession of popes is infallible.[46] As a matter of fact, it is true that the ordinary papal teaching is precisely the means of handing on the same unchanging faith of the Roman Church. Nevertheless, the 'per se' infallibility of each individual act of ordinary and universal papal teaching which proposes a doctrine in a definitive way must be defended.

A distinction between the papacy and the pope, or between the Holy See (*sedes*) and the one sitting in the See (*sedens*), was sharply drawn and utilized by the great Bossuet against the infallibility of the pope at the 1682 Assembly of the Gallican Clergy. In conversation with Bishop Choiseul of Tournai, Bossuet argues that: "The faith of this See is indeed indefectible; nevertheless its judgments are not infallible."[47] Bossuet knew that the indefectibility of the faith of the Roman Church could not be denied, and so he tried to allow for this while still denying the infallibility of the individual Roman pontiffs. His opponent accused him of inconsistency in this, since the indefectibility of the Roman Church already implies the infallibility of the Roman pontiff: for if it were possible for even one pope to teach error or heresy in a manner binding the assent of the faithful, then the Roman Church itself would thereby fall into error or heresy.[48] This

---

[46] Paul Nau, O.S.B., "An Essay on the Authority of the Teachings of the Sovereign Pontiff," in *Pope or Church? Essays on the Infallibility of the Ordinary Magisterium*, trans. Arthur E. Slater (Kansas City: Angelus Press, 1998), 12–19.

[47] Reported by Fenelon, and cited by Henry Edward Manning, *The Centenary of Saint Peter and the General Council: A Pastoral Letter to the Clergy* (London: Longmans, Green, and Co., 1867), 42.

[48] Bishop Choiseul: "If that be so . . . absolute infallibility is ascribed not indeed to the man who sits in the See, but to the See itself. And so it must be admitted that every decree which emanates from the Apostolic See is altogether irreformable, and confirmed by infallible authority" (Manning, *The Centenary of Saint Peter*, 42).

question of a distinction between 'sedes' and 'sedens' was also addressed by Gasser at Vatican I:

"In what sense can the infallibility of the Roman Pontiff be said to be *personal*? It is said to be *personal* in order to exclude in this way a distinction between the Roman Pontiff and the Roman Church. Indeed, infallibility is said to be personal in order thereby to exclude a distinction between the See and the one who holds the See. Since this distinction did not acquire any patrons in the general congregations, I shall refrain from saying anything about it. Therefore, having rejected the distinction between the Roman Church and the Roman Pontiff, between the See and the possessor of the See, that is, between the universal series and the individual Roman Pontiffs succeeding each other in this series, we defend the personal infallibility of the Roman Pontiff inasmuch as this prerogative belongs, by the promise of Christ, to each and every legitimate successor of Peter in his chair."[49]

Nau's position resurrects this same distinction, so vigorously rejected by Bishop Gasser, between the individual pope and the series of popes, and applies it to the ordinary papal magisterium, although not to the extraordinary.

Now, it is generally the case that doctrines proposed as definitive by the ordinary papal magisterium are taught by many popes in succession, and this is one of three principal means of identifying definitive ordinary teaching. But the important point is that there should not be any need to search out how many times a doctrine has been taught or by how many popes in order to conclude that it has been taught infallibly if it has been set forth even once in such words or in such a document as to manifest that,

---

[49] Gasser, *The Gift of Infallibility*, 41: "Quo in sensu infallibilitas Romani pontificis dicenda est *personalis*? Dicenda est *personalis* ut sic excludatur distinctio inter Romanum pontificem et Romanam ecclesiam. Porro infallibilitas dicitur personalis, ut sic excludatur distinctio inter sedem et sedentem. Cum haec distinctio in congregationibus generalibus nullos nacta fuerit patrones, etiam de iis aliquid addendo supercedeo. Reiecta ergo distinctione inter ecclesiam Romanam et Romanum pontificem, inter sedem et sedentem, id est, inter seriem universam et inter singulos Romanos pontifices in hac serio sibi succedentes, defendimus personalem Romani pontificis infallibilitatem eatenus, quatenus haec praerogativa omnibus et singulis legitimis Petri in cathedra euis successoribus ex Christi promissione competit" (Msi 52:1212).

according to the mind and will of that pope, the doctrine is to be held definitively. Nau's position essentially equates the infallibility of the ordinary papal magisterium with the inerrancy of the entire tradition of the Roman Church, which is the same as its indefectibility. On the contrary, I submit that infallibility is a quality proper to individual acts, and that it is precisely the infallibility of individual acts of ordinary papal teaching which guarantees the indefectibility of the Roman Church.

CHAPTER FOUR

INFALLIBLE DEFINITIONS 'EX CATHEDRA'

Having established by speculative argumentation that the pope speaks infallibly not only in his solemn judgments, but also in his ordinary and universal teaching, when he proposes a doctrine of faith or morals as definitively to be held by the whole Church, we may now turn to considerations of positive magisterial teaching, beginning with the interpretation of the Vatican I definition as it pertains to the ordinary and extraordinary papal magisterium. Following upon this, particular attention will be given to the very interesting problem posed by several statements pronounced by Pope John Paul II in *Ordinatio sacerdotalis* and in *Evangelium vitae*. Finally, although we cannot attempt a fresh survey of all the historical possibilities, we will conclude with a discussion of some examples of infallible papal teaching, both ordinary and extraordinary.

a) The Chair of Truth

Although the common opinion now is that Vatican I defined the infallibility only of the extraordinary papal magisterium, there have been authors, such as Fenton, who hold that both ordinary definitions and solemn judgments are included in the meaning of the Vatican definition. In fact, Fenton notes it as a matter of interest that there are some authors (Dublanchy and Salaverri included) who hold the opposite position.[1]

We have already found that the ordinary and universal teaching of the pope is infallible when he proposes a doctrine of

---

[1] Fenton, "Infallibility in the Encyclicals," 181; "The doctrinal Authority of Papal Encyclicals," 214.

faith and morals as to be held definitively. The question now is whether the word 'defines' in the text of the definition of papal infallibility means anything other than or more than just this. Let us listen to Bishop Gasser explain the meaning of 'defines' and 'definition' as they are intended to be understood in the definition of infallibility. In his major '*relatio*' of July 11, Gasser describes what a definition is in these words:

> "Not just any manner of proposing the doctrine is sufficient even when he is exercising his office as supreme pastor and teacher. Rather, there is required the manifest intention of defining doctrine, either of putting an end to a doubt about a certain doctrine or of defining a thing, [by] giving a definitive judgment and proposing that doctrine as one which must be held by the Universal Church. This last point is indeed something intrinsic to every dogmatic definition of faith or morals which is taught by the supreme pastor and teacher of the Universal Church and which is to be held by the Universal Church. Indeed this very property and note of a definition, properly so-called, should be expressed, at least in some way, since he is defining doctrine to be held by the Universal Church."[2]

When he summarizes the contents of the definition later in the speech, he describes a definition as follows:

> "The Roman Pontiff, through the divine assistance promised to him, is infallible, when, by his supreme authority, he defines a doctrine which

---

[2] Gasser, *The Gift of Infallibility*, 74: "Secundo non sufficit quivis modus proponendi doctrinam, etiam dum pontifex fungitur munere supremi pastoris et doctoris, sed requiritur intentio manifestata definiendi doctrinam, seu fluctuationi finem imponendi circa doctrinam quamdam seu rem definiendam, dando definitivam sententiam, et doctrinam illam proponendo tenendam ab ecclesia universali. Hoc ultimum est quidem aliquid intrinsecum omni definitioni dogmaticae de fide vel moribus, quae docentur a supremo pastore et doctore ecclesiae universalis et ab universa ecclesia tenenda: verum hanc propietatem ipsam et notam definitionis proprie dictae aliquatenus saltem etiam debet exprimere, cum doctrinam ab universali ecclesia tenendam definit" (Msi, 52:1225).

must be held by the Universal Church, or, as very many theologians say, when he definitively and conclusively proposes his judgment."[3]

Then, on July 16, after the fathers had submitted their observations on the text and their recommendations for amendment, Gasser responded with a lengthier statement on the intended meaning of the word 'defines':

"My second observation concerns the word 'define' as it is found in our Draft. It is obvious from the many exceptions that this word is an obstacle for some of the reverend fathers; hence, in their exceptions, they have completely eliminated this word or have substituted another word, viz., 'decree,' or something similar, in its place, or have said simultaneously, 'defines and decrees,' etc. Now I shall explain in a very few words how this word 'defines' is to be understood according to the Deputation *de fide*. Indeed, the Deputation *de fide* is not of the mind that this word should be understood in a juridical sense (Lat. *in sensu forensi*) so that it only signifies putting an end to controversy which has arisen in respect to heresy and doctrine which is properly speaking *de fide*. Rather, the word 'defines' signifies that the Pope directly and conclusively pronounces his sentence about a doctrine which concerns matters of faith or morals and does so in such a way that each one of the faithful can be certain of the mind of the Apostolic See, of the mind of the Roman Pontiff; in such a way, indeed, that he or she knows for certain that such and such a doctrine is held to be heretical, proximate to heresy, certain or erroneous, etc., by the Roman Pontiff. Such, therefore, is the meaning of the word 'defines.'"[4]

---

[3] Ibid., 78: "Romanum pontificem per promissam sibi divinam assistentiam esse infallibilem, cum pro suprema sua auctoritate doctrinam ab universa ecclesia tenendam definit seu, ut plures theologi loquuntur, definitiva ac terminativa sententia proponit" (Msi, 52: 1227).

[4] Gasser, *The Gift of Infallibility*, 73–74: "Secunda animadversio concernit verbum 'definit' in formula nostra. Ex exceptionibus pluribus patet, quod verbum istud quibusdam reverendissimis patribus scrupulum iniiciat; proinde aut omnino verbum istud in suis exceptionibus deleverunt, aut aliud, scilicet *decernit* aut quid simile substituerunt, aut simul dixerunt *definit et decernit* etc. Iam paucissimis verbis dicam, quomodo a Deputatione de fide verbum istud *definit* sit accipiendum. Utique Deputatio de fide non in ea mente est, quod verbum istud debeat sumi in sensu forensi, ut solummodo significet finem impositum controversiae, quae de haeresi et de doctrina quae proprie est de fide,

The description of the act of infallible ordinary teaching found in *Lumen gentium* is 'teaching a sentence as definitively to held' (*docentes sententiam tamquam definitive tenendam*).[5] If the same must be said of uniquely papal magisterium as of the general ecclesiastical magisterium, then the infallibility of the ordinary papal magisterium is found whenever the pope, acting as supreme head of the universal Church, teaches or proposes a sentence as definitively to be held. Compare this description of ordinary infallible papal teaching to Gasser's various descriptions of infallible papal definitions: 'defining doctrine' (*definiendi doctrinam*), 'putting an end to doubt about some doctrine' (*fluctuationi finem imponendi circa doctrinam quamdam*), 'defining a thing' (*rem definiendam*) by 'giving a definitive sentence' (*dando definitivam sententiam*) and by 'proposing that doctrine as to be held by the universal Church' (*et doctrinam illam proponendo tenendam ab ecclesia universali*). The pope defines doctrine when he 'definitively and conclusively proposes his sentence' (*definitiva ac terminativa sententia proponit*), or when he 'directly and conclusively profers his sentence' (*suam sententiam circa doctrinam directe et terminative proferat*).

Hence, if the word 'defines' is accepted as meaning what Gasser says that it means, then it is hard to avoid the conclusion that a teaching act of the ordinary papal magisterium, by which the pope proposes a doctrinal sentence as definitively to be held by the whole Church, does in fact constitute an '*ex cathedra*' definition in the sense intended by the First Vatican Council. To interpret the scope of '*ex cathedra*' definitions as intended to be inclusive of ordinary conclusive papal sentences, and not only solemn

---

agitata fuit; sed vox *definit* significat, quod papa suam sententiam circa doctrinam, quae est de rebus fidei et morum, directe et terminative proferat, ita ut iam unusquisque fidelium certus esse possit de mente sedis apostolicae, de mente Romani pontificis; ita quidem ut certo sciat a Romano pontifice hanc vel illam doctrinam haberi haereticam, haeresi proximam, certam vel erroneam, etc." (Msi, 52:1316).

[5] Vatican II, *Lumen gentium*, § 25; cited above, p. 55, n. 11.

judgments or extraordinary definitions, is also the only way to make sense of Gasser's protestation: "Already thousands and thousands of dogmatic judgments have gone forth from the Apostolic See."[6] Even allowing for hyperbole, it would be hard to take this as referring only to solemn or extraordinary judgments. Of these many authors now find only two, and even the more generous counts of former times did not find more than a dozen.

Further support for the inclusion of ordinary definitions within the scope of the Vatican definition may be found in papal usage of the phrase 'ex cathedra'. Like the chair of Moses (Mt 23:2), the chair of Peter symbolizes not only extraordinary but also ordinary teaching authority: the chair of Peter is the chair of truth. Pope Pius IX speaks thus in his first encyclical letter, just months after his elevation to the papacy: "We, therefore, placed inscrutably by God upon this Chair of truth (*in hac veritatis Cathedra*). . ."[7] He reminds the bishops that the magisterium judges infallibly all questions of faith and morals, and that this infallible magisterium lives and acts in the Church founded on Peter; he then continues:

> "And the Church is where Peter is, and Peter speaks in the Roman Pontiff, living at all times in his successors and making judgment, providing the truth of the faith to those who seek it. The divine words therefore mean what this Roman See of the most blessed Peter (*haec Romana Beatissimi Petri Cathedra*) holds and has held. For this mother and teacher of all the churches has always preserved entire and unharmed the faith entrusted to it by Christ the Lord. Furthermore, it has taught it to the faithful, showing all men truth and the path of salvation."[8]

---

[6] Gasser, *The Gift of Infallibility*, 47: "Iam millena et millena iudicia dogmatica a sede apostolica emanerunt" (Msi, 52: 1215).

[7] Pope Pius IX, Encyclical Letter on Faith and Religion *Qui pluribus* (9 Nov. 1846), § 12, in PE, vol. 1, 279: "Nos igitur, qui inscrutabili Dei judicio in hac veritatis Cathedra collocati sumus . . ." (*Pii IX Pontificis Maximi Acta* I, vol. 1 [Rome: Typographia Bonarum Artium, 1854], 11).

[8] Ibid., § 10–11, in PE, vol. 1, 279: "Et quoniam ubi Petrus ibi Ecclesia, ac Petrus per Romanum Pontificem loquitur, et semper in suis successoribus vivit, et judicium exercet, ac praestat quaerentibus fidei veritatem, idcirco divina

Pope Leo XIII speaks similarly in his own first encyclical letter. The chair of Peter, in his words, is the 'chair of truth and justice', and the 'apostolic seat of truth'. The pope addresses his brother bishops with this urgent plea:

"We here call upon you, venerable brothers, with particular earnestness, and strongly urge you to kindle, with priestly zeal and pastoral care, the fire of the love of religion among the faithful entrusted to you, that their attachment to this chair of truth and justice (*huic Cathedrae veritatis et justitiae*) may become closer and firmer, that they may welcome all its teachings with thorough assent of mind and will, wholly rejecting such opinion, even when most widely received, as they know to be contrary to the Church's doctrine. In this matter, the Roman Pontiffs, Our predecessors, and the last of all, Pius IX, of sacred memory, especially in the General Council of the Vatican, have not neglected, so often as there was need, to condemn widespreading errors and to smite them with the apostolic condemnation. . . . All such censures, We, following in the steps of Our predecessors, do confirm and renew from this apostolic seat of truth (*ex hac Apostolica veritatis Sede*)."[9]

---

eloquia eo plane sensu sunt accipienda, quem tenuit ac tenet haec Romana Beatissimi Petri Cathedra, quae omnium Ecclesiarum mater et magistra fidem a Christo Domino traditam, integram inviolatamque semper servavit, eamque fideles edocuit, omnibus ostendens salutis semitam, et incorruptae veritatis doctrinam" (*Pii IX Acta* I, vol. 1, p. 10).

[9] Pope Leo XIII, Encyclical Letter on the Evils of Society *Inscrutabili Dei consilio* (21 Apr. 1878), § 13: "Vos hoc loco peculiari cum affectu appellamus, Venerabiles Fratres, et vehementer hortamur, ut pro sacerdotali zelo et pastorali vigilantia Vestra fideles Vobis creditos religionis amore incendatis, quo propius et arctius huic Cathedrae veritatis et justitiae adhaereant, omnes ejus doctrinas intimo mentis et voluntatis assensu suscipiant; opiniones vero etiam vulgatissimas, quas Ecclesiae documentis oppositas noverint omnino rejiciant. Qua in re Romani Pontifices Decessores Nostri, ac demum sa. me. Pius IX, praesertim in oecumenico Vaticano Concilio prae oculis habentes verba Pauli . . . haud praetermiserunt, quoties opus fuit, grassantes errores reprobare et apostolica censura confodere. Has condemnationes omnes, Decessorum Nostrorum vestigia sectantes, Nos ex hac Apostolica veritatis Sede confirmamus ac iteramus" (*Lettres Apostoliques de S. S. Léon XIII*, vol. 1 [Paris: Maison de la Bonne, 1890], 18).

Pope Pius XII, in an encyclical letter promoting devotion to the Sacred Heart of Jesus, also refers to the chair of Peter as 'the chair of truth'. After mentioning certain people denigrating devotion to the Sacred Heart, the pope inquires: "Who does not see, venerable brethren, that opinions of this kind are in entire disagreement with the teachings which Our predecessors officially proclaimed from this seat of truth (*ex hac veritatis cathedra*) when approving the devotion to the Sacred Heart of Jesus?"[10]

What kind of teachings are these of which Pope Pius XII says that they have been published from the chair of truth? It is nothing other than the ordinary teaching found in papal encyclical letters. He explicitly references encyclical letters of Pope Leo XIII and Pope Pius XI, in neither of which is there any sign of an extraordinary definition or solemn judgment.[11] Vatican I defines the infallibility of the pope when he speaks '*ex cathedra*'. It then explains that he speaks '*ex cathedra*' when he defines, etc. Now Pius XII says that the pope speaks '*ex cathedra*' in these encyclical letters. Since these encyclical letters do not appear to contain extraordinary definitions, this implies that they must contain ordinary definitions, and hence that ordinary papal definitions are '*ex cathedra*' definitions in the relevant sense. Solemn papal definitions and ordinary papal definitions come forth from the same chair of Peter, the same chair of truth; and infallibility is nothing other than the charism of certain truth.

This explanation of the proper interpretation of Vatican I with regard to the act of infallible papal teaching also renders the interpretation of *Lumen gentium* less difficult with regard to ordinary papal teaching and religious submission. The document

---

[10] Pope Pius XII, Encyclical Letter on Devotion to the Sacred Heart *Haurietis aquas* (15 May 1956), § 14: "Quis non videat, Venerabiles Fratres, opinationes eiusmodi a sententiis omnino discrepare, quas Decessores Nostri, Sacratissimi Cordis Iesu cultum comprobantes, ex hac veritatis cathedra publice ediderunt?" (AAS 48 [1956]: 313).

[11] Pope Leo XIII, Encyclical Letter on Consecration to the Sacred Heart *Annum sacrum* (25 May 1899); Pope Pius XI, Encyclical Letter on Reparation to the Sacred Heart *Miserentissimus Redemptor* (8 May 1928).

says that religious submission of will and intellect is due to the teaching of the pope even when he is not speaking '*ex cathedra*'.[12] If the meaning of speaking '*ex cathedra*' is limited to extraordinary definitions, then this would mean that religious submission is due to all of the teaching of the ordinary papal magisterium. Since this kind of religious submission is generally understood to imply an ultimately conditional assent such as is only properly given to teachings which have not been proposed infallibly, this text of *Lumen gentium* may be taken to imply the fallibility of the ordinary papal magisterium altogether. One possible solution is to highlight the word 'also' and to interpret the declaration that religious submission is 'also' to be given to ordinary papal teaching as implying that religious submission is also to be given to extraordinary teaching so that it has a general sense which does not exclude a firm and definitive assent. A more elegant solution, however, would be to interpret the '*ex cathedra*' locution referred to here as already inclusive of ordinary papal definitions, which could be plausible for the reasons already mentioned, so that religious submission is restricted exclusively to merely authoritative non-infallible teaching.

b) Ordinatio sacerdotalis and Evangelium vitae

Several definitive statements made by Pope John Paul II, first in the Apostolic Letter *Ordinatio sacerdotalis* (1994), and then also in the Encyclical Letter *Evangelium vitae* (1995), have given rise to a great deal of discussion about their exact nature and doctrinal authority.[13] The statement in *Ordinatio sacerdotalis* regards the

---

[12] Vatican II, *Lumen gentium*, § 25: "Hoc vero religiosum voluntatis et intellectus obsequium singulari ratione praestandum est Romani pontificis authentico magisterio etiam cum non ex cathedra loquitur" (DEC, 869).

[13] See Francis A. Sullivan, S.J., "New Claims for the Pope," *The Tablet* 248 (18 Jun. 1994): 767–69; "The Doctrinal Weight of *Evangelium vitae*," *Theological Studies* 56 (1995): 560–65; "Recent Theological Observations on Magisterial Documents and Public Dissent," *Theological Studies* 58 (1997): 509–15; *Creative Fidelity*, 181–84; Angel Antón, "*Ordinatio Sacerdotalis*: Algunas reflexiones de 'gnoseología teológica'," *Gregorianum* 75 (1994): 723–

reservation of priestly ordination to men alone. At the conclusion of his letter, Pope John Paul II makes the following declaration:

> "Wherefore, in order that all doubt may be removed regarding a matter of great importance, a matter which pertains to the Church's divine constitution itself, in virtue of my ministry of confirming the brethren (cf. Lk 22:32) I declare that the Church has no authority whatsoever to confer priestly ordination on women and that this judgment is to be definitively held by all the Church's faithful."[14]

From a comparison of this declaration with the conditions enumerated by Vatican I this would appear to be a clear case of an infallible definition 'ex cathedra':

Pastor Aeternus	*Ordinatio sacerdotalis*
'in the exercise of his office as shepherd and teacher of all Christians,'	The document is addressed to all the bishops of the Church.
'in virtue of his supreme apostolic authority,'	'in virtue of my ministry of confirming the brethren'
he defines	'in order that all doubt may be removed . . . I declare that'
A doctrine concerning faith or morals	'a matter which pertains to the Church's divine constitution itself,'
to be held by the whole Church,	'this judgment is to be definitively held by all the Church's faithful.'
he possesses . . . infallibility	?

42; Peter Hünermann, "Schwerwiegende Bedenken: Eine Analyse des Apostolischen Schreibens 'Ordinatio Sacerdotalis'," *Herder Korrespondenz* 48 (1994): 406–10; Gaillardetz, "The Ordinary Universal Magisterium," 449–52.

[14] Pope John Paul II, Apostolic Letter *Ordinatio sacerdotalis* (22 May 1994), 4: "Ut igitur omne dubium auferatur circa rem magni momenti, quae ad ipsam Ecclesiae divinam constitutionem pertinet, virtute ministerii Nostri confirmandi fratres (cf. *Lc* 22, 32), declaramus Ecclesiam facultatem nullatenus habere ordinationem sacerdotalem mulieribus conferendi, hancque sententiam ab omnibus Ecclesiae fidelibus esse definitive tenendam" (AAS 86 [1994]: 548).

1. *Adequate subject of infallibility:* The document is addressed to all the bishops of the Church, and using the royal plural, the pope invokes his ministry of confirming the brethren (Lk 22:32). Not only is this Lukan passage one of the three *loci classici* on which the dogma of papal infallibility is founded, it is also cited explicitly by *Lumen gentium* in its reformulation of the doctrine.[15]

2. *Adequate object of infallibility*: The matter of the declaration pertains to the divine constitution of the Church, which is at least instrinsically connected with divine revelation.

3. Adequate act of infallibility: The declaration itself is explicitly intended to remove all doubt about the matter (*Ut igitur omne dubium auferatur*) by proposing a sentence as definitively to be held by all the faithful (*hancque sententiam ab omnibus Ecclesiae fidelibus esse definitive tenendam*). According to Gasser's explanation, for an infallible definition: 'there is required the manifest intention of defining doctrine' (*requiritur intentio manifestata definiendi doctrinam*). This may be an intention 'either of putting an end to a doubt about a certain doctrine' (*seu fluctuationi finem imponendi circa doctrinam quamdam*) 'or of defining a thing' (*seu rem definiendam*). This is accomplished 'by giving a definitive sentence' (*dando definitivam sententiam*) 'and by proposing that doctrine as to be held by the whole Church' (*et doctrinam illam proponendo tenendam ab ecclesia universali*).[16]

---

[15] Vatican II, *Lumen gentium*, § 25: "The Roman pontiff, head of the college of bishops, by virtue of his office, enjoys this infallibility when, as supreme shepherd and teacher of all Christ's faithful, who confirms his brethren in the faith (see Lk 22, 32), he proclaims in a definitive act a doctrine on faith or morals" (DEC, 869).

[16] Gasser, *The Gift of Infallibility*, 74: "Secundo non sufficit quivis modus proponendi doctrinam, etiam dum pontifex fungitur munere supremi pastoris et doctoris, sed requiritur intentio manifestata definiendi doctrinam, seu fluctuationi finem imponendi circa doctrinam quamdam seu rem definiendam, dando definitivam sententiam, et doctrinam illam proponendo tenendam ab ecclesia universali. Hoc ultimum est quidem aliquid intrinsecum omni definitioni dogmaticae de fide vel moribus, quae docentur a supremo pastore et

If it is the case, therefore, as it appears to be, that this declaration is an infallible definition '*ex cathedra*' in the sense intended by Vatican I, then one is left with two choices: one can either (1) affirm that this declaration is an extraordinary solemn definition, or (2) hold that it remains an act of the ordinary papal magisterium while simultaneously admitting that the infallibility of the ordinary papal magisterium in its definitive teaching is positively taught in the definition of Vatican I.

Now Cardinal Ratzinger, who as prefect of the CDF at that time was presumably in a good position to know the mind and intention of Pope John Paul II in this matter, explains this declaration as an expression of the ordinary papal magisterium. In connection with a response of the CDF to a dubium submitted about the doctrine contained in *Ordinatio sacerdotalis*,[17] Ratzinger published his own commentary in *L'Osservatore Romano*:

> "In response to this precise act of the Magisterium of the Roman Pontiff . . . all members of the faithful are required to give their assent to the teaching stated therein. To this end, the Congregation for the Doctrine of the Faith, with the approval of the Holy Father, has given

---

doctore ecclesiae universalis et ab universa ecclesia tenenda: verum hanc propietatem ipsam et notam definitionis proprie dictae aliquatenus saltem etiam debet exprimere, cum doctrinam ab universali ecclesia tenendam definit" (Msi, 52:1225).

[17] Congregation for the Doctrine of the Faith, Responsum ad Propositum Dubium concerning the Teaching Contained in "*Ordinatio Sacerdotalis*" (28 Oct. 1995): "*Dubium*: Whether the teaching that the Church has no authority whatsoever to confer priestly ordination on women, which is presented in the Apostolic Letter *Ordinatio Sacerdotalis* to be held definitively, is to be understood as belonging to the deposit of faith. *Responsum*: Affirmative. This teaching requires definitive assent, since, founded on the written Word of God, and from the beginning constantly preserved and applied in the Tradition of the Church, it has been set forth infallibly by the ordinary and universal Magisterium (cf. Second Vatican Council, Dogmatic Constitution on the Church *Lumen Gentium* 25, 2). Thus, in the present circumstances, the Roman Pontiff, exercising his proper office of confirming the brethren (cf. Lk 22:32), has handed on this same teaching by a formal declaration, explicitly stating what is to be held always, everywhere, and by all, as belonging to the deposit of the faith."

an official Reply on the nature of this assent; it is a matter of full definitive assent, that is to say, irrevocable, to a doctrine taught infallibly by the Church. . . . It should be emphasized that the definitive and infallible nature of this teaching of the Church did not arise with the publication of the Letter *Ordinatio Sacerdotalis*. In the Letter . . . the Roman Pontiff . . . has confirmed the same teaching by a formal declaration. . . . In this case, an act of the ordinary Papal Magisterium, in itself not infallible, witnesses to the infallibility of the teaching of a doctrine already possessed by the Church."[18]

This is a very difficult statement. It appears that Ratzinger makes three assertions which cannot easily be understood as fully compatible with one another: (1) the assent of the faithful is required in response to this precise act of the papal magisterium; (2) the nature of this assent must be full, definitive, and irrevocable; (3) this precise act of the papal magisterium is, in itself, not infallible (i.e. fallible). It seems hard to avoid the conclusion that the faithful are thus said to owe a full and irrevocable assent precisely in response to a fallible act of teaching, which is surely incredible.

Nevertheless, there are two distinct claims to be considered here: (1) that the declaration is an act of the ordinary papal magisterium rather than a solemn definition; and (2) that, as such, it is fallible in itself. With regard to the first point, an earlier article, which Ratzinger had published in *L'Osservatore Romano* shortly after the promulgation of the Apostolic Letter itself, helps to illuminate his line of thought:

"In view of a magisterial text of the weight of the present Apostolic Letter, inevitably another question is raised: how binding is this document? It is explicitly stated that what is affirmed here must be definitively held in the Church, and that this question is no longer open to the interplay of differing opinions. Is this therefore an act of dogmatizing? Here one must answer that the Pope is not proposing any new dogmatic formula, but is confirming a certainty which has been constantly lived and held firm in the Church. In the technical language one should say: here we have an act of the ordinary Magisterium of the

---

[18] Joseph Ratzinger, "Letter Concerning the CDF Reply Regarding *Ordinatio Sacerdotalis*," *L'Osservatore Romano* (19 Nov. 1995).

Supreme Pontiff, an act therefore which is not a solemn definition *ex cathedra*, even though in terms of content a doctrine is presented which is to be considered definitive. In other words, a certainty already existing in the Church, but now questioned by some, is confirmed by the Pope's apostolic authority. It has been given a concrete expression, which also puts in a binding form what has always been lived."[19]

Looking closely at both of the above statements of Ratzinger, it seems that he understands solemn definitions of the extraordinary magisterium to involve necessarily the proposing of *new* dogmatic formulae.[20] That is, he appears to infer the ordinary character of this act of teaching from the fact that no new precision or formulation or clarification of doctrine is present here. Only the same doctrine, already infallibly taught by the ordinary and universal magisterium of the bishops, is again emphatically declared by the pope. The distinguishing characteristic of the extraordinary magisterium is the introduction of something new in the doctrine of the Church: either a new qualification of a doctrine such as occurs when a doctrine is dogmatized, or a new precision or formulation of a doctrine such as was introduced by the words '*homoousion*' with respect to the Incarnation, or '*transubstantiatio*' regarding the Eucharist.

However, if one follows Ratzinger on this point, which seems quite reasonable, then one must also admit not only that the ordinary papal magisterium is infallible, but that its infallibility has been positively defined by the First Vatican Council. The real problem in Ratzinger's explanation of the declaration of *Ordinatio sacerdotalis* is not that he classifies it as act of ordinary papal teaching, but that he presumes that this implies its fallibility. To be sure, he argues forcefully that the doctrine itself is infallibly taught by the ordinary and universal magisterium of the bishops, which includes the pope; but he denies that there is in the declaration of Pope John Paul II an exercise of a personal and distinct infallibility, which by itself calls for assent (*assensum per se*

---

[19] Joseph Ratzinger, "The Limits of Church Authority," *L'Osservatore Romano* (29 Jun. 1994): 7.

[20] Italics added for emphasis.

postulare),[21] and issues in a doctrinal definition which is of itself irreformable (*ex sese irreformabilis*),[22] at least in the sense of being irrevocable.

The most unfortunate result of Ratzinger's statement is that many theologians have felt free to regard the declaration of Pope John Paul II as the authoritative but essentially fallible opinion of the pope (and the response of the CDF as a likewise authoritative but essentially fallible opinion) about a disputed question of fact: namely, whether the bishops in their state of dispersion throughout the world have unanimously agreed in proposing the impossibility of ordaining women as a doctrine to be held definitively. And such a conclusion is notoriously difficult to establish.

Regarding the central point, however, the weight of probability which attaches to Ratzinger's opinions due to his position in Rome is counter-balanced by the opinion of Archbishop Bertone, who was the secretary of the CDF at the time and therefore Ratzinger's closest collaborator. Bertone agrees with Ratzinger in explaining the declaration as an act of the ordinary papal magisterium, but he comes to the opposite conclusion with regard to the more important point of its infallibility. He writes:

> "It seems a pseudo-problem to wonder whether this papal act of 'confirming' a teaching of the ordinary, universal Magisterium is infallible or not. In fact, although it is not 'per se' a 'dogmatic definition' (like the Trinitarian dogma of Nicaea, the Christological dogma of Chalcedon or the Marian dogmas), a papal pronouncement of confirmation enjoys the same infallibility as the teaching of the ordinary, universal Magisterium, which includes the Pope not as a mere Bishop but as the Head of the Episcopal College."[23]

According to Bertone, then, the papal act of confirmation of a doctrine already taught infallibly by the ordinary and universal magisterium of the bishops is also itself infallible. The ordinary

---

[21] Pius XII, *Humani generis*, § 20; cited above, p. 63, n. 33.

[22] Vatican I, *Pastor Aeternus*, cap. 4; cited above, p. 1, n. 3.

[23] Bertone, "Magisterial Documents and Public Dissent," *L'Osservatore Romano* (29 Jan. 1997).

and universal teaching of the pope, which here takes the form of a confirmation of a doctrine already held and taught in the Church, enjoys the same infallibility as the ordinary and universal magisterium of the episcopal body, of which the pope is the head. The distinct infallibility of the papal act of confirmation is not brought out here as clearly as could be desired, but the essential point is made.

An additional discussion of the three outstanding pronouncements of John Paul II in the Encyclical Letter *Evangelium vitae* (1995) would run along precisely the same lines, for which reason we may just sketch the question in outline. The first exceptionally definitive statement confirms the grave immorality of murder:

> "Therefore, by the authority which Christ conferred upon Peter and his Successors, and in communion with the Bishops of the Catholic Church, I confirm that the direct and voluntary killing of an innocent human being is always gravely immoral. This doctrine, based upon that unwritten law which man, in the light of reason, finds in his own heart (cf. Rom 2:14–15), is reaffirmed by Sacred Scripture, transmitted by the Tradition of the Church and taught by the ordinary and universal Magisterium."[24]

The second statement declares the grave immorality of direct abortion:

> "Therefore, by the authority which Christ conferred upon Peter and his Successors, in communion with the Bishops – who on various occasions have condemned abortion and who in the afore-mentioned consultation, albeit dispersed throughout the world, have shown

---

[24] Pope John Paul II, Encyclical Letter on the Value and Inviolability of Human Life *Evangelium vitae* (3 Mar. 1995), § 57: "Quapropter Nos auctoritate usi Petro euisque Successoribus a Christo collata, coniuncti cum Ecclesiae catholicae Episcopis, *confirmamus directam voluntariamque hominis innocentis interfectionem graviter inhonestam esse semper*. Doctrina haec, cuius innituntur radices illa in non scripta lege quam, praeeunte rationis lumine, quivis homo suo reperit in animo (cfr *Rom* 2, 14–15), inculcatur denuo Sacris in Litteris, Ecclesiae Traditione commendatur, atque ordinario et universali Magisterio explanatur" (AAS 87 [1995]: 465).

unanimous agreement concerning this doctrine – I declare that direct abortion, that is, abortion willed as an end or as a means, always constitutes a grave moral disorder, since it is the deliberate killing of an innocent human being. This doctrine is based upon the natural law and upon the written Word of God, is transmitted by the Church's Tradition and taught by the ordinary and universal Magisterium."[25]

Finally, a third statement confirms the grave immorality of euthanasia:

> "Taking into account these distinctions, in harmony with the Magisterium of my Predecessors and in communion with the Bishops of the Catholic Church, I confirm that euthanasia is a grave violation of the law of God, since it is the deliberate and morally unacceptable killing of a human person. This doctrine is based upon the natural law and upon the written word of God, is transmitted by the Church's Tradition and taught by the ordinary and universal Magisterium."[26]

Once again, the conditions set forth at Vatican I appear to be met. The pope acts as pastor and teacher in relation to the universal Church, solemnly invokes his supreme apostolic authority, and issues his definitive sentence on three moral doctrines. Nevertheless, the doctrinal commentary issued by Ratzinger and Bertone on the concluding formula of the *Professio fidei* implies

---

[25] John Paul II, *Evangelium vitae*, § 62: "Auctoritate proinde utentes Nos a Christo Beato Petro euisque Successoribus collata, consentientes cum Episcopis qui abortum crebrius respuerunt quique in superius memorata interrogatione licet per orbem disseminati una mente tamen de hac ipsa concinuerunt doctrina – *declaramus abortum recta via procuratum, sive uti finem intentum seu ut instrumentum, semper gravem prae se ferre ordinis moralis turbationem*, quippe qui deliberata exsistat innocentis hominis occisio. Haec doctrina naturali innititur lege Deique scripto Verbo, transmittitur Ecclesiae Traditione atque ab ordinario et universali Magisterio exponitur" (AAS 87 [1995]: 472).

[26] Ibid., § 65: "His rite interpositis distinctionibus, Magisterium Nos Decessorum Nostrorum iterantes atque in communione cum catholicae Ecclesiae Episcopis *confirmamus euthanasiam gravem divinae Legis esse violationem*, quatenus est conscia necatio personae humanae, quae moraliter probari non potest. Haec doctrina lege naturali atque Verbo Dei scripto adnixa, Ecclesiae Traditione traducitur atque Magisterio ordinario et universali explicatur" (AAS 87 [1995]:477).

that these are ordinary acts of papal teaching rather than solemn definitions. This commentary addresses the possibility, thrice realized in *Evangelium vitae*, that the pope may formally confirm a doctrine already proposed infallibly by the ordinary and universal magisterium of the bishops.[27] Here, too, it is said that an explicit and formal confirmation by the pope of a truth already taught by the ordinary and universal magisterium of the bishops is not to be considered a solemn definition. Once again, this is unproblematic only if one concedes that such a confirmation or declaration is nonetheless an infallible '*ex cathedra*' definition, albeit an ordinary one.

c) Particular Cases of Infallible Papal Teaching

Since the definition of the First Vatican Council, there have been only a few attempts to catalogue the historical instances of solemn papal definitions and there have been no attempts to catalogue the vastly more numerous ordinary papal definitions, although Dublanchy and Cartechini provide a few examples.

The first attempts at creating lists of solemn papal definitions, although not claiming to be exhaustive, were made by Louis Billot and by Edmond Dublanchy, each of whom includes

---

[27] CDF, *Doctrinal Commentary*, § 9: "In the case of a *non-defining* act, a doctrine is taught *infallibly* by the ordinary and universal Magisterium of the Bishops dispersed throughout the world who are in communion with the Successor of Peter. *Such a doctrine can be confirmed or reaffirmed by the Roman Pontiff, even without recourse to a solemn definition*, by declaring explicitly that it belongs to the teaching of the ordinary and universal Magisterium as a truth that is divinely revealed (first paragraph) or as a truth of Catholic doctrine (second paragraph). Consequently, when there has not been a judgement on a doctrine in the solemn form of a definition, but this doctrine, belonging to the inheritance of the *depositum fidei*, is taught by the ordinary and universal Magisterium, which necessarily includes the Pope, such a doctrine is to be understood as having been set forth infallibly. The declaration of *confirmation* or *reaffirmation* by the Roman Pontiff in this case is not a new dogmatic definition, but a formal attestation of a truth already possessed and infallibly transmitted by the Church."

eleven examples.[28] More recently, the Catholic participants of the Lutheran-Roman Catholic Dialogue (LRCD) in the United States took up the question and concluded that there were only two.[29] The Jesuit theologian and historian Klaus Schatz made a more thorough study, the results of which are taken up approvingly by Sullivan.[30] He recognizes seven solemn papal definitions. Finally, the CDF has offered some examples, also not intended to be exhaustive, in its commentary on the *Professio fidei*.[31] Here is a chart for the sake of comparison, with check marks (√) to indicate affirmation of a solem papal definition, demonstrating how opinions vary on this subject:

Pope / Doctrine	Billot	Dublanchy	Schatz	LRCD	CDF
449. Pope St Leo I. The union of two natures in Christ: *Lectis dilectionis*.	√	√	√		
680. Pope St Agatho. The existence of two wills and two operations in Christ: *Omnium bonorum spes*.		√	√		
1302. Pope Boniface VIII. The necessity for salvation of submission to the Roman Pontiff: *Unam sanctam*.	√	√			

---

[28] Billot, *Tractatus de Ecclesia Christi*, 642–44; Dublanchy, "Infaillibilité," 1703–4.

[29] Lutheran-Roman Catholic Dialogue, "Teaching Authority and Infallibility in the Church," *Theological Studies* 40 (1979): 148.

[30] Klaus Schatz, S.J., "Welche bisherigen päpstlichen Lehrentscheidungen sind 'ex cathedra'? Historische und theologische Überlegungen," in *Dogmengeschichte und katholische Theologie*, ed. Werner Löser, Karl Lehmann, and Matthias Lutz-Bachmann (Würzburg: Echter, 1985), 402–22; cf. Sullivan, *Creative Fidelity*, 82–89.

[31] CDF, *Doctrinal Commentary*, § 11.

Pope / Doctrine	Billot	Dublanchy	Schatz	LRCD	CDF
1520. Pope Leo X. Condemnation of the errors of Luther (Lutheranism): *Exsurge Domine.*	√	√			
1653. Pope Innocent X. Condemnation of five propositions of Jansen (Jansenism): *Cum occasione.*	√	√	√		
1687. Pope Innocent XI. Condemnation of the errors of Molinos (Quietism): *Caelestis Pastor.*	√	√			
1699. Pope Innocent XII. Condemnation of the errors of Fenelon (Semi-Quietism): *Cum alias.*	√	√			
1713. Pope Clement XI. Condemnation of the errors of Quesnel (Jansenism): *Unigenitus.*	√	√			
1794. Pope Pius VI. Condemnation of the errors of the Synod of Pistoia (Jansenism and Gallicanism): *Auctorem fidei.*	√	√	√		
1854. Pope Pius IX. The immaculate conception of the Blessed Virgin Mary: *Ineffabilis Deus.*	√	√	√	√	√

Pope / Doctrine	Billot	Dublanchy	Schatz	LRCD	CDF
1896. Pope Leo XIII. The invalidity of Anglican ordinations: *Apostolicae curae.*					√
1950. Pope Pius XII. The bodily assumption of the Blessed Virgin Mary into heaven: *Munificentissimus Deus.*			√	√	√

The LRCD document considers various possibilities – the solemn canonization of saints, the condemnations of Jansenism and Modernism, the condemnation of Luther (particularly relevant to their dialogue), the condemnations of contraception, and the invalidity of Anglican orders – before ultimately rejecting them all as candidates for infallible teaching. Their method, however, is highly dubious. Appealing to the juridical principle which says that, "Nothing is to be understood as dogmatically declared or defined unless this is clearly manifest,"[32] the authors go on to claim that, "For the infallible character to be clearly manifest, the condemnation would have to claim infallibility for itself."[33] Such a criterion is wholly without justification, not to mention anachronistic, though it can claim for itself a pedigree from John Henry Newman.[34] What is necessary for infallible teaching is not

---

[32] LRCD, "Teaching Authority and Infallibility," 149. The citation is from the then current *Code of Canon Law* (1917), can. 1323, § 3; cf. *Code of Canon Law* (1983), can. 749, §3: "No doctrine is understood as defined infallibly unless this is manifestly evident."

[33] LRCD, "Teaching Authority and Infallibility," 149.

[34] In his celebrated letter to the Duke of Norfolk, Newman seeks to defend the newly promulgated dogma with respect to the case of Pope Honorius by arguing that this pope's letter to the patriarch of Constantinople was not an *ex cathedra* definition. "I say so first," he writes, "because he could not fulfil the above conditions of an *ex cathedrâ* utterance, if he did not actually *mean* to fulfil them . . . and who will dream of saying . . . that Honorius in the 7th century

that it should be presented as infallible, but that it should be presented as definitive.

With such a criterion it is a wonder that the LRCD members found even two infallible definitions.[35] As it is, however, we can accept without further difficulty, in addition to *Munificentissimus Deus* (1950)[36] and *Ineffabilis Deus* (1854),[37] the equally clear cases of *Benedictus Deus* (1336)[38] and *Unam sanctam* (1302),[39] as infallible papal definitions.

---

did actually intend to exert that infallible teaching voice which has been dogmatically recognized in the nineteenth?" (Newman, *Letter to the Duke of Norfolk*, 108).

[35] The authors claim, with reference to the Immaculate Conception and the Assumption, that, "These definitions, contained in apostolic constitutions published in the form of bulls, are phrased in unmistakably solemn language . . . and clearly claim to be infallibly uttered" (LRCD, "Teaching Authority and Infallibility," p. 148, n. 106), but in fact even these do not claim to be infallible in any explicit way. Rather, it is their very extraordinary definitiveness which clearly implies their infallibility.

[36] Pope Pius XII, Apostolic Constitution *Munificentissimus Deus* (1 Nov. 1950), § 44: "By the authority of our Lord Jesus Christ, of the Blessed Apostles, Peter and Paul, and by Our own authority We pronounce, declare, and define that the dogma was revealed by God, that the Immaculate Mother of God, the ever Virgin Mary, after completing her course of life upon earth, was assumed to the glory of heaven both in body and in soul" (D 2333).

[37] Pope Pius IX, Bull *Ineffabilis Deus* (8 Dec. 1854): "By the authority of our Lord Jesus Christ, of the Blessed Apostles, Peter and Paul, and by Our own, We declare, pronounce, and define that the doctrine, which holds that the most Blessed Virgin Mary at the first instance of her conception, by a singular grace and privilege of Almighty God, in virtue of the merits of Christ Jesus, the Savior of the human race, was preserved immaculate from all stain of original sin, has been revealed by God, and on this account must be firmly and constantly believed by all the faithful" (D 1641).

[38] Pope Benedict XII, Bull *Benedictus Deus* (29 Jan. 1336): "By this edict which will prevail forever, with apostolic authority we declare: that according to the common arrangment of God, souls of all the saints . . . immediately after their death and that aforesaid purgation in those who were in need of a purgation of this kind, even before the resumption of their bodies and the general judgment after the ascension of our Savior, our Lord Jesus Christ, into heaven, have been, are, and will be in heaven, in the kingdom of heaven and in celestial paradise with Christ, united in the company of the holy angels, and after the passion and death of our Lord Jesus Christ have seen and see the divine essence by intuitive

Although Schatz accepts *Benedictus Deus* as an infallible definition, he still denies *Unam sanctam* on the grounds that its teaching has not been 'received' by the Church.[40] Similarly, it is the positive 'reception' of the Tome of Pope St Leo the Great by the Council of Chalcedon (451),[41] and of the dogmatic letter of Pope St Agatho by the Council of Constantinople III (680–681),[42] that leads him to include these in his list of solemn '*ex cathedra*' definitions. Sullivan is sensitive to the fact that the rejection of *Unam sanctam* on these grounds appears to be a negation of the '*ex sese*' clause of the Vatican I definition, which asserts, against the Gallican doctrine, that papal definitions are "of themselves, and not by the consent of the Church, irreformable."[43] He attempts to defend this approach by recalling that:

> "The pope can define as dogma only a truth that is revealed, and that must therefore be contained at least implicitly in the faith of the Church. The eventual failure of any papal doctrine to be received by the Church as an article of its faith would show that the doctrine was not contained in the deposit of faith, and hence was not capable of being defined as dogma."[44]

This is a complete inversion of the proper relationship between

---

vision, and even face to face, with no mediating creature, serving in the capacity of an object seen, but divine essence immediately revealing itself plainly, clearly, and openly, to them" (D 530).

[39] Pope Boniface VIII, Bull *Unam sanctam* (18 Nov. 1302): "Furthermore, we declare, say, define, and proclaim to every human creature that they by necessity for salvation are entirely subject to the Roman Pontiff" (D 469).

[40] See the discussion of Sullivan, *Creative Fidelity*, 85–89; cf. Francis A. Sullivan, S.J., *Salvation Outside the Church? Tracing the History of the Catholic Response* (Eugene, Ore.: Wipf and Stock, 2002), 63–66.

[41] Pope St Leo I, Letter to Flavian of Constantinople *Lectis dilectionis* (13 Jun. 449); DEC, 77–82; D 143–44; Council of Chalcedon, Session V, Definition of Faith *Sancta et magna* (22 Oct. 451); DEC, 83–87; D 148.

[42] Pope St Agatho, Letter to Constantine IV *Omnium bonorum spes* (680); D 288; Council of Constantinople III, Session XVIII, Exposition of Faith *Unigenitus Dei* (16 Sep. 681); DEC, 124–30; D 289–93.

[43] Vatican I, *Pastor Aeternus*, cap. 4 (DEC, 816); cited above, p. 1, n. 3.

[44] Sullivan, *Creative Fidelity*, 88.

faith and authority. Sullivan would have it that the authoritativeness of a papal definition should be judged by the beliefs and tenets of the faithful, rather than that these should be defined by a papal judgment. It is true, of course, as Vatican II teaches in *Lumen gentium*, that "the assent of the Church . . . can never fail to be given to these definitions,"[45] and yet it may be that the rejection of a papal definition, even by a great number of Catholics, manifests their separation from the Church rather than the *sensus fidei* of the Church.

Of the fourteen cases listed above, seven take the form of solemn condemnations of errors. Of these, Schatz retains only two – *Auctorem fidei* (1794)[46] and *Cum occasione* (1653),[47] excluding the others because they do not condemn propositions distinctly as heretical. Instead, they employ global censures, on account of which Sullivan agrees with Schatz that:

> "Since this form of censure does not explicitly condemn any particular proposition as heretical, one cannot conclude that the contradictory of any of the condemned propositions is a defined dogma. Such

---

[45] Vatican II, *Lumen gentium*, § 25: "Istis autem definitionibus assensus ecclesiae numquam deesse potest propter actionem eiusdem Spiritus sancti, qua universus Christi grex in unitate fidei servatur et proficit" (DEC, 870).

[46] Pope Pius VI, Bull *Auctorem fidei* (28 Aug. 1794): "Implorato itaque cum assiduis nostris tum et piorum christifidelium privatis publicisque precibus Spiritus sancti lumine, omnibus plene et mature consideratis, complures ex actis et decretis memoratae synodi propositiones, doctrinas, sententias, sive expresse traditas, sive per ambiguitatem insinuatas, suis ut praefatum est, cuique appositis notis et censuris damnandas et reprobandas censuimus, prout hac nostra perpetuo valitura constitutione damnamus et reprobamus" (Msi 38:1264). Ninety-nine propositions are then individually condemned as heretical, erroneous, etc. (D 1501–99).

[47] Pope Innocent X, Bull *Cum occasione* (31 May 1653), § 4: "Cum autem ab initio huiuscemodi discussionis, ad divinum implorandum auxilium, multorum Christi fidelium preces tum privatim tum publice indixissemus, postmodum iteratis eisdem ferventius, ac per nos sollicite imploratâ Sancti Spiritus assistentiâ, ad infrascriptas devenimus declarationem et definitionem" (BR[T], vol. 15, 720). Each of the five propositions are individually condemned as heretical (D 1092–96).

documents, therefore, are to be seen as examples of the ordinary, non-definitive exercise of papal magisterium."[48]

What Schatz and Sullivan overlook here is the fact that papal infallibility extends to the secondary object of the magisterium. What is necessary is only that the propositions be defined as erroneous, or contrary to truths of Catholic doctrine. This appears to be the case at least with regard to *Exsurge Domine* (1520), which censures the forty-one condemned errors of Martin Luther as "respectively heretical, or scandalous, or false, or offensive to pious ears, or seductive of simple minds, and in opposition to Catholic truth."[49] The final censure (*veritati catholicae obviantes*), which is introduced with 'and' instead of 'or', is what may render its inclusion possible. The same problem of global condemnation makes it difficult to judge also in the cases of *Unigenitus* (1713),[50] *Cum alias* (1699),[51] and *Caelestis Pastor* (1687).[52]

---

[48] Sullivan, *Creative Fidelity*, 89.

[49] Pope Leo X, Bull *Exsurge Domine* (15 Jun. 1520), § 4: "De eorundem itaque venerabilium fratrum nostrorum consilio, & assensu, ac omnium, & singulorum praedictorum matura deliberatione praedicta, auctoritate Omnipotens Dei, & beatorum Apostolorum Petri, & Pauli, & nostra, praefatos omnes, & singulos articulos seu errores, tanquam, ut praemittitur, respective haereticos, aut scandalosos, aut falsos, aut piarum aurium offensivos, vel simpliciu mentium seductivos, & veritati catholicae obviantes, damnamus, reprobamus, atque omnino rejicimus, ac pro damnatis, reprobatis, & rejectis ab omnibus utriusque sexus Christi fidelibus haberi debere, harum serie decernimus, & declaramus" (MBR, vol. 1, 615); D 781.

[50] Pope Clement XI, Bull *Unigenitus* (8 Sep. 1713): One hundred and one propositions of Pasquier Quesnel are "declared and condemned as false, captious, evil-sounding, offensive to pious ears, scandalous, pernicious, rash, injurious to the Church and her practice, insulting not only to the Church but also to the secular powers, seditious, impious, blasphemous, suspected of heresy, and smacking of heresy itself, and, besides, favoring heretics and heresies, and also schisms, erroneous, close to heresy, many times condemned, and finally heretical, clearly renewing many heresies respectively and most especially those which are contained in the infamous propositions of Jansen, and indeed accepted in that sense in which these have been condemned" (D 1451).

[51] Pope Innocent XII, Brief *Cum alias* (12 Mar. 1699). Twenty-three propositions of Fenelon are "condemned and rejected as, either in the obvious

104

Quanta cura (1864) is an easier case, since "all and each evil opinion and doctrine individually mentioned in this letter" are simply and utterly condemned.[53] And to oblige all the faithful to hold these evil opinions "as absolutely rejected, proscribed, and condemned (*veluti reprobatas, proscriptas atque damnatas omnino*)"[54] is equivalent to proposing their opposites as truths of Catholic doctrine "to be held definitively (*definitive tenendam*)."[55]

Finally, the inclusion of *Apostolicae curae* (1896) by the CDF provides an excellent case in point of a definition of a truth which clearly belongs to the secondary object of the magisterium, for the invalidity of a particular, historical rite of ordination is certainly not contained directly in the deposit of faith.[56] This may

---

sense of these words, or in the extended meaning of the thoughts, rash, scandalous, ill-sounding, offesive to pious ears, pernicious, and likewise erroneous in practice" (D 1349).

[52] Pope Innocent XI, Bull *Caelestis Pastor* (20 Nov. 1687). Sixty-eight propositions of Miguel de Molinos are "condemned as heretical, suspect, erroneous, scandalous, blasphemous, offensive to pious ears, rash, of relaxed Christian discipline, subversive, and seditious respectively" (D 1288).

[53] Pope Pius IX, Encyclical Letter Condemning Current Errors *Quanta cura* (8 Dec. 1864): "In such great perversity of evil opinions, therefore, We, truly mindful of Our Apostolic duty, and especially solicitous about our most holy religion, about sound doctrine and the salvation of souls divinely entrusted to Us, and about the good of human society itself, have decided to lift Our Apostolic voice again. And so all and each evil opinion and doctrine individually mentioned in this letter, by Our Apostolic authority We reject, proscribe, and condemn; and We wish and command that they be considered as absolutely rejected, proscribed, and condemned by all the sons of the Catholic Church" (D 1699).

[54] Pius IX, *Quanta cura* (ASS 3 [1867]: 166).

[55] Vatican II, *Lumen gentium*, § 25; cited above, p. 55, n. 11.

[56] Pope Leo XIII, Bull *Apostolicae curae* (15 Sep. 1896): "And so, assenting entirely to the decrees of the departed Pontiffs in this case, and confirming them most fully, and, as it were, renewing them by Our authority, of Our own inspiration and certain knowledge We pronounce and declare that ordinations enacted according to the Anglican rite have hitherto been and are invalid and utterly void" (D 1966). Cf. CDF, *Doctrinal Commentary*, § 11: "With regard to those truths connected to revelation by historical necessity and which are to be held definitively, but are not able to be declared as divinely revealed, the following examples can be given: the legitimacy of the election of

thus be taken as an additional confirmation of the thesis of the extension of papal infallibility to the secondary object of the magisterium.

With regard to ordinary papal teaching, Dublanchy provides some examples of infallible teaching taken entirely from the acts of Pope Leo XIII:

a) In the Encyclical *Arcanum*, of 10 February 1880, on Christian marriage: the divine institution of the sacrament of marriage, the indissolubility of marriage, and the exclusive and integral power of the Church over Christian marriage.

b) In the Encyclical *Diuturnum*, of 29 June 1881: the divine origin of power residing in civil society, a truth taught as clearly attested in the holy Scriptures and in the monuments of Christian antiquity.

c) In the Encyclical *Immortale Dei*, of 1 November 1885: the sovereign independence of the Church, which possesses, in virtue of its divine institution, full and absolute authority in all matters which are hers.

d) In the Encyclical *Providentissimus Deus*, of 18 November 1893: particularly these two teachings concerning the holy Books: the Catholic notion of their inspiration and the absence of all error in the sacred text faithfully preserved.

e) In the Encyclical *Satis cognitum*, of 29 June 1896: all the catholic doctrine on the papal primacy, which is proposed as defined and universally accepted doctrine in the Church.[57]

---

the Supreme Pontiff or of the celebration of an ecumenical council, the canonizations of saints (*dogmatic facts*), the declaration of Pope Leo XIII in the Apostolic Letter *Apostolicae Curae* on the invalidity of Anglican ordinations."

[57] My translation of Dublanchy, "Infaillibilité," 1705: "Comme exemples d'enseignement infaillible du magistère ordinaire du pape nous indiquerons particulièrement, dans les encycliques de Léon XIII, les enseignements suivants: *a*) Dans l'encyclique *Arcanum,* du 10 février 1880, sur le mariage chrétien, la divine institution du sacrement de mariage, l'indissolubilité du mariage et le pouvoir exclusif et intégral de l'Église sur le mariage chrétien. – *b*) Dans l'encyclique *Diuturnum,* du 29 juin 1881, l'origine divine du pouvoir résidant dans la société civile, vérité enseignée comme évidemment attestée dans la sainte Écriture et dans les monuments de l'antiquité chrétienne. – *c*) Dans l'encyclique *Immortale Dei*, du 1er novembre 1885, la souveraine indépendance de l'Église qui possède, en vertu de son institution divine, pleine et absolue

The defining characteristic of each of these examples is that they are presented by the pope to the whole Church, without any particular solemnity or invocations of supreme authority, as truths of faith or morals which are either divinely revealed or at least theologically certain in connection with divine revelation. Cartechini adds the dogmatic truths taught in the Athanasian Creed,[58] the Formula of Pope Hormisdas,[59] the Tridentine Profession of Pope Pius IV,[60] and the Anti-Modernist Oath,[61] as further examples of infallible ordinary papal teaching.[62]

Perhaps the most important examples of infallible ordinary papal teaching, however, are the repeated condemnations of contraception. One of the most important consequences of the acceptance of the infallibility of the ordinary papal magisterium would be the termination of the seemingly endless controversies over the status of the doctrine of the sinful nature of contraception. Pope Pius IX condemned the use of contraception in no uncertain terms in the Encyclical Letter *Casti connubii* (1930):

> "Since, therefore, openly departing from the uninterrupted Christian tradition some recently have judged it possible solemnly to declare another doctrine regarding this question, the Catholic Church, to whom God has entrusted the defense of the integrity and purity of morals, standing erect in the midst of the moral ruin which surrounds her, in order that she may preserve the chastity of the nuptial union from being defiled by this foul stain, raises her voice in token of her divine

---

autorité en toutes les matières qui sont siennes. – *d*) Dans l'encyclique *Providentissimus Deus*, du 18 novembre 1893, particulièrement ces deux enseignements concernant les Livres saints: la notion catholique de leur inspiration et l'absence de toute erreur dans le texte sacré fidèlement conservé. – *e*) Dans l'encyclique *Satis cognitum*, du 29 juin 1896, toute la doctrine catholique sur la primauté pontificale qui y est proposée comme doctrine définie et universellement reconnue dans l'Église."

[58] The Creed *Quicumque vult*; D 39–40.

[59] Pope St Hormisdas, *Libellus professionis fidei*, appended to the Epistle to the Bishops of Spain *Inter ea quae* (2 Apr. 517); D 171–72.

[60] Pope Pius IV, Bull *Iniunctum nobis* (13 Nov. 1565); D 994–1000.

[61] Pope St Pius X, Apostolic Letter Motu Proprio *Sacrorum antistitum* (1 Sep. 1910); D 2145–47.

[62] Cartechini, *De valore notarum theologicarum*, I, cap. 4.

ambassadorship and through Our mouth proclaims anew: any use whatsoever of matrimony exercised in such a way that the act is deliberately frustrated in its natural power to generate life is an offense against the law of God and of nature, and those who indulge in such are branded with the guilt of a grave sin."[63]

A few decades later, after much anticipation and speculation as to whether the Church could or would change her teaching on this matter, Pope Paul VI re-confirmed it in the Encyclical Letter *Humanae vitae* (1968):

"Therefore We base Our words on the first principles of a human and Christian doctrine of marriage when We are obliged once more to declare that the direct interruption of the generative process already begun and, above all, all direct abortion, even for therapeutic reasons, are to be absolutely excluded as lawful means of regulating the number of children. Equally to be condemned, as the magisterium of the Church has affirmed on many occasions, is direct sterilization, whether of the man or of the woman, whether permanent or temporary. Similarly excluded is any action which either before, at the moment of, or after sexual intercourse, is specifically intended to prevent procreation – whether as an end or as a means."[64]

---

[63] Pope Pius XI, Encyclical Letter on Christian Marriage *Casti connubii* (31 Dec. 1930), § 56: "Cum igitur quidam, a christiana doctrina iam inde ab initio tradita neque umquam intermissa manifesto recedentes, aliam nuper de hoc agendi modo doctrinam sollemniter praedicandam censuerint, Ecclesia Catholica, cui ipse Deus morum integritatem honestatemque docendam et defendendam commisit, in media hac morum ruina posita, ut nuptialis foederis castimoniam a turpi hac labe immunem servet, in signum legationis suae divinae, altam per os Nostrum extollit voc em atque denuo promulgat: quemlibet matrimonii usum, in quo exercendo, actus, de industria hominum, naturali sua vitae procreandae vi destituatur, Dei et naturae legem infringere, et eos qui tale quid commiserint gravis noxae labe commaculari" (AAS 22 [1930]: 560).

[64] Pope Paul VI, Encyclical Letter on the Regulation of Birth *Humanae vitae* (25 Jul. 1968), § 14: "Quare primariis hisce principiis humanae et christianae doctrinae de matrimonio nixi, iterum debemus edicere, omnino respuendam esse, ut legitimum modum numeri liberorum temperandi, directam generationis iam coeptae interruptionem, ac praesertim abortum directum, quamvis curationis causa factum. Pariter, sicut Ecclesiae Magisterium pluries docuit, damnandum est seu viros seu mulieres directo sterilitate, vel perpetuo vel ad tempus, afficere. Item quivis respuendus est actus, qui, cum coniugale

Only a few authors have argued that one or the other or both of these condemnations are infallible papal definitions.[65] The more common opinion is that they are examples of ordinary papal teaching, and as such presumably fallible in themselves; thus defenders of the irreformability of the Church's teaching on this point have mostly striven to prove that the doctrine has been infallibly taught by the ordinary and universal magisterium of the bishops dispersed throughout the world teaching in union with the pope.[66] It is of the nature of such teaching, however, as their opponents have ceaselessly pointed out, that it is difficult in the extreme to conclude to its infallibility with any great degree of certitude.[67] The acceptance of the above papal condemnations of

---

commercium vel praevidetur vel efficitur vel ad suos naturales exitus ducit, id tamquam finem obtinendum aut viam adhibendam intendat, ut procreatio impediatur" (AAS 60 [1968]: 490).

[65] For example, Felix Cappello, S.J., *De matrimonio*, vol. 5 of *Tractatus canonico-moralis de sacramentis iuxta Codicem juris canonici*, 7th ed. (Turin; Rome: Marietti, 1961), no. 816; Francis Ter Haar, C.SS.R., *De praecipuis hujus aetatis vitiis eorumque remediis*, vol. 2 of *Casus conscientiae* (Turin; Rome: Marietti, 1939), no. 136; Brian W. Harrison, O.S., "The *Ex Cathedra* Status of the Encyclical *Humanae Vitae*," *Living Tradition* 43 (Sep.–Nov. 1992); Ermenegildo Lio, *Humanae Vitae e Infallibilità: il Concilio, Paolo VI e Giovanni Paolo II* (Vatican City: Libreria Editrice Vaticana, 1986). Lio received an autograph letter of thanks for this work from Pope John Paul II.

[66] The pre-eminent example of this is the work of John C. Ford and Germain Grisez, "Contraception and the Infallibility of the Ordinary Magisterium," *Theological Studies* 39 (1978): 258–312.

[67] See Garth L. Hallett, S.J., "Contraception and Prescriptive Infallibility," *Theological Studies* 43 (1982): 629–50; Germain Grisez, "Infallibility and Contraception: A Reply to Garth Hallett," *Theological Studies* 47 (1986): 134–45; Garth Hallet, S.J., "Infallibility and Contraception: The Debate Continues," *Theological Studies* 49 (1988): 517–28; Sullivan, *Magisterium*, 143–48; Grisez, "Infallibility and Specific Moral Norms," 248–87; Sullivan, "The 'Secondary Object' of Infallibility," 543–50; Germain Grisez, "The Ordinary Magisterium's Infallibility," *Theological Studies* 55 (1994): 720–32; Francis A. Sullivan, S.J., "The Ordinary Magisterium's Infallibility: A Reply to Germain Grisez," *Theological Studies* 55 (1994): 732–37; Germain Grisez, "Response to Francis Sullivan's Reply," *Theological Studies* 55 (1994): 737–38; Lawrence J. Welch, "The Infallibility of the Ordinary Universal Magisterium: A Critique of Some Recent Observations," *Heythrop Journal* 39 (1998): 18–36; Gaillardetz, "The

contraception as infallible of themselves, even if only as ordinary definitive teaching rather than as extraordinary solemn definitions, would bring any and all such debate swiftly to its conclusion. Indeed, one may well wonder whether this is in itself a considerable factor behind the widespread denial of the infallibility of the ordinary papal magisterium.

Ordinary Universal Magisterium," *Theological Studies* 63 (2002): 447–71; Lawrence J. Welch, "Reply to Richard Gaillardetz on the Ordinary Universal Magisterium and to Francis Sullivan," *Theological Studies* 64 (2003): 598–609; Francis A. Sullivan, S.J., "Reply to Lawrence J. Welch," *Theological Studies* 64 (2003): 610–15.

CONCLUSION

In the first part of this work I set out to defend the thesis that: the infallibility of the papal magisterium extends not only to divinely revealed dogmas of faith or morals (*de fide divina et catholica credenda*), but also to each and every secondary truth of Catholic doctrine pertaining to faith or morals (*de fide definitive tenenda*). The two questions at play here are the theological qualification of the thesis of the infallibility of the pope with regard to the secondary object and the precise scope or extension of the secondary object itself. Since the First Vatican Council clearly established that the same is to be said of the papal magisterium as is said of the Church's magisterium with regard to the object of infallibility, we have not confined ourselves to dealing only with texts that specifically address the object of papal infallibility.

After reviewing and carefully interpreting the definition of the First Vatican Council in light of the official explanations of Bishop Gasser, we encountered influential interpreters who have understood the matter quite differently. Francis Sullivan, one of the most prominent authors treating of the subject in the late twentieth century, explicitly disagrees with my thesis on both points. He claims:

> "In any case, it is important to recall that the magisterium has never definitively settled the question whether it can speak definitively about matter that is not in the deposit of revelation, and still less has it settled definitively the question as to the limits of such an object of infallible teaching."[68]

Regarding the first point, we have seen the doctrine clearly proposed as certainly true by Vatican I in the dogmatic constitution *Pastor Aeternus*, by Vatican II in the dogmatic constitution *Lumen gentium*, by two important documents of the Congregation for the Doctrine of the Faith (*Mysterium Ecclesiae* and *Donum veritatis*),

---

[68] Sullivan, "The Theologian's Ecclesial Vocation," 56.

111

and by the *Catechism of the Catholic Church.* The doctrine is also codified in the law of the Church, both East and West. Although I grant that this doctrine has not been solemnly defined by an extraordinary judgment, I maintain that its presence and character in the aforementioned documents is sufficient to conclude that it has been definitively taught by the ordinary and universal magisterium. It pertains to the second paragraph of the *Professio fidei* as a truth of Catholic doctrine which is to be held definitively by Catholic or ecclesiastical faith (*de fide definitive tenenda*).

With regard to the second point, which is the extension of the secondary object itself to each and every truth pertaining to faith or morals, including the entire natural law and its specific moral norms, we have discovered a variety of formulations of the secondary object. Vatican I uses the generic formula 'doctrine of faith or morals' (*doctrinam de fide vel moribus*) in order to include the secondary object; Vatican II alludes to the secondary object in its reference to the deposit of faith, 'to be guarded inviolate and expounded faithfully' (*sancte custodiendum et fideliter exponendum*). The CDF on one occasion describes the secondary object as containing those things 'without which this deposit could not be rightly guarded and expounded' (*sine quibus hoc depositum rite nequit custodiri et exponi*); on another occasion it speaks merely of things 'intimately connected' (*intime conectuntur*) or 'strictly and intimately connected' (*stricte et intime conectuntur*) to divine revelation. The Catechism utilizes variations of all of these, and the *Professio fidei* returns to the original language of Vatican I: 'doctrine of faith or morals' (*circa doctrinam de fide vel moribus*).

Rather than seeing broader or stricter limits of the secondary object in any of these various formulations, I maintain that they must be equivalent. In order to be able to hold each statement as true and consistent, one must first of all hold with Bishop Gasser that the infallibility of the Church extends to the entire genus of 'faith and morals'. Secondly, one must accept as an explanation of this extension of infallibility the fact that each and every non-revealed truth which pertains to faith and morals is required for the protection and explanation of the deposit of faith on account of its strict and intimate connection with it; and in fact, this requirement is the very basis of the connection. With regard to morals in particular, each and every moral doctrine is necessarily connected with divine revelation through being connected to man's final end, which he moves toward or away from through all his good or evil actions. It makes nonsense of Vatican I to say that the Church (and therefore also the pope) is infallible in its teaching on matters of faith and morals, and then to say that there is a species of moral teaching about which the Church cannot teach infallibly.

In the second part of this work I then defended the thesis that: the pope speaks infallibly not only in his solemn judgments or definitions (*de fide divina et catholica credenda*), but also in his ordinary and universal teaching, when he proposes a doctrine of faith or morals as definitively to be held by the whole Church (*sententia fidei proxima*). This follows as a speculative conclusion from two fundamental premises. The first and major premise is that the pope individually possesses the charism of infallibility in its fullness. This is implied in the definition of papal infallibility where doctrine of faith and morals is said to be the object of papal infallibility in the same way and to the same extent as it is the object of episcopal infallibility. It is even more clearly implied in the definition of supreme papal jurisdiction, where it is defined that the pope possesses the total plenitude of supreme power in the Church. And it is clearly stated in *Lumen gentium* that the pope individually possesses the same charism of infallibility possessed by the Church.

The minor premise simply states the clearly taught and universally acknowledged fact that the bishops of the Church, as a collective body, are able to teach infallibly both in their solemn definitions, which can only occur at ecumenical councils, and in their ordinary and universal teaching, which can also occur even when they are dispersed throughout the world. This is strongly implied at Vatican I in *Dei Filius* and explicitly taught by Vatican II in *Lumen gentium*. The conclusion follows that the pope can also speak infallibly in his ordinary and universal magisterium. Since

113

the two premises are divinely revealed truths, the conclusion is also materially a dogma, although not proposed explicitly as such by the Church. As such, it is proximate to the faith (*sententia fidei proxima*). The notes by which infallible ordinary papal teaching can be recognized are the same as those specified for the ordinary infallible teaching of the bishops, namely, that they or he should propose a doctrine of faith or morals as definitively to be held by the whole Church. This, I have argued, is properly to be understood as equivalent to proposing a doctrine as theologically certain, as opposed to merely safe or probable teaching which is essentially opinionative, albeit still authoritative.

In the final chapter we considered whether the infallibility of the ordinary papal magisterium may actually be included positively in the Vatican definition of papal infallibility. The explanations of Gasser and the reference of Pius XII to the ordinary teaching of encyclical letters as 'publically published from this chair of truth' (*ex hac veritatis cathedra publice ediderunt*) appear to support this minority interpretation. The insistence of Ratzinger and Bertone on the ordinary character of John Paul II's declarations and confirmations in *Ordinatio sacerdotalis* and *Evangelium vitae* lend further support to this contention, although in an unusual fashion. The formulation of the declaration in *Ordinatio sacerdotalis* in particular, read in light of the definition of papal infallibility in *Pastor Aeternus* and the recapitulation of the same doctrine in *Lumen gentium*, leads to an inescapable dilemma: (1) either this declaration is a solemn extraordinary definition and thus infallible, or (2) it is an ordinary papal definition, the infallibility of which was thus positively declared at Vatican I. The conclusion that it is an infallible papal definition '*ex cathedra*' follows in either case.

Finally, an overview of some of the most prominent examples of infallible papal teaching, both ordinary and extraordinary, made possible a concrete application of the principles and conclusions previously discovered. Indeed, it is at this level that the theses defended herein, if accepted, stand to exercise the greatest influence both on theology and on the life of the Church at large. To name but a few of the most outstanding examples, the absolute inerrancy of Scripture will have to be accepted as infallibly taught in a way which contradicts the common interpretation of Vatican II's Constitution *Dei Verbum*; the use of contraception will have to be accepted as infallibly condemned, making dissent of any kind entirely illegitimate and punishable under canon law; and the whole tradition of definitive papal teaching on religious liberty and the rights and duties of states vis-à-vis God and the Church must be acknowledged as infallible, thus raising the stakes considerably in the difficult but urgent task of reconciling Vatican II's Declaration *Dignitatis humanae* with the whole Catholic tradition so as to achieve the necessary interior reconciliation within the heart of the Church.

POST-SCRIPT
CORRECTIONS AND FURTHER
COMMENTS

A short time after this thesis had already been successfully presented and defended before the faculty of the International Theological Institute, it was subjected to an additional round of criticism, for which I am very grateful. Some new objections were raised that allowed me to see more clearly certain aspects of the questions under consideration. Therefore, I would like to make some corrections and add some further comments here.

1. Divine and Ecclesiastical Faith

It was objected that the first part of the thesis makes frequent use of the distinction between divine and ecclesiastical faith without sufficient reference to its ultimate inadequacy. That is to say, although the distinction between the primary and secondary object of the magisterium is certainly valid, and the assent given in each case does differ, it would be a mistake to suppose that divine and ecclesiastical faith are mutually exclusive. For, of course, faith in the Church's teaching (ecclesiastical faith) is ultimately grounded in the belief that God constituted the Church as an authoritative teacher (divine faith).

2. Vatican I on the Secondary Object

With regard to the principal argument of Chapter One, it should be re-iterated that the First Vatican Council does not explicitly teach that either the pope or the Church is infallible with regard to the secondary object of the magisterium. The argument intends to say only that this is sufficiently implied in the teaching set forth there.

3. Opposing Arguments

One objection states that I was sometimes unjust in the consideration given to opposing arguments, citing as an example a discussion on page 37 of Francis Sullivan's treatment of the Schema on the Church prepared for Vatican II. It seems that I addressed only one of his arguments, whereas he had made two. Since I no longer have Sullivan's work on hand, I have not been able to verify this for myself, but assuming that it is correct, I can only say that it was certainly not my intention to misrepresent or mistreat either my opponents or their arguments.

4. The Second Paragraph of the Profession of Faith

On page 50 of the thesis, the sentence has been changed which previously read: "Apropos of the present discussion, it appears from the second paragraph that each and every (*omnia et singula*) doctrine which has to do with faith or morals (*circa doctrinam de fide vel moribus*) is able to be definitively proposed by the Church." It was rightly objected that this contains a formally invalid argument, since a universal affirmative is not convertible. The paragraph in question states that every doctrine definitively proposed by the Church is to be accepted, but it does not follow that every doctrine is able to be definitively proposed. Hence, the sentence now reads: "Apropos of the present discussion, the second paragraph presents the object of infallibility simply as 'doctrine of faith or morals' (*doctrinam de fide vel moribus*)."

5. Religious Submission of Will and Intellect

The paragraph on papal infallibility in *Lumen gentium* 25 says that the pope is infallible when he speaks 'ex cathedra' (presumably using this phrase in the same sense intended by Vatican I), apparently meaning that he is infallible only when he speaks 'ex cathedra' since a religious submission of will and intellect is generally understood to be called for by non-infallible authoritative teaching. At the same time, however, I do not think that this is absolutely conclusive, since it would seem to me that a definitive assent such as is due to infallible teaching could still be accurately described as a religious submission of will and intellect. That is, this latter description could be generic enough to describe both definitive and non-definitive assent. In any case, the interpretation proposed still seems possible inasmuch as the text does not distinguish explicitly between ordinary and extraordinary papal teaching, but only between 'ex cathedra' and non-'ex cathedra' teaching. But further research into the sense of that phrase as understood and intended by the fathers of the Second Vatican Council would certainly be worth undertaking.

6. Archbishop Bertone's Interpretation of *Ordinatio sacerdotalis*

A paragraph previously found on pages 88–89 has been deleted which discussed the interpretation of Archbishop Tarcisio Bertone with regard to the infallibility of *Ordinatio sacerdotalis*. Bertone agrees with Ratzinger in explaining this declaration of Pope John Paul II as an act of the ordinary papal magisterium, and then has this to say about the question of its infallibility:

> "It seems a pseudo-problem to wonder whether this papal act of 'confirming' a teaching of the ordinary, universal Magisterium is infallible or not. In fact, although it is not 'per se' a 'dogmatic definition' (like the Trinitarian dogma of Nicaea, the Christological dogma of Chalcedon or the Marian dogmas), a papal pronouncement of confirmation enjoys the same infallibility as the teaching of the ordinary, universal Magisterium, which includes the Pope not as a mere Bishop but as the Head of the Episcopal College."[69]

Whereas I had interpreted Bertone to be saying that the act of papal confirmation is infallible just as the previous acts of universal episcopal teaching were infallible, his words could also be read to mean (and perhaps this is more likely) that the papal act is

---

[69] Bertone, "Magisterial Documents and Public Dissent," *L'Osservatore Romano* (29 Jan. 1997).

infallible only by its participation in the universal episcopal teaching, and hence that it is not in itself infallible. Hence, I do not assert that Bertone's interpretation of *Ordinatio sacerdotalis* with regard to its infallibility differs essentially from Cardinal Ratzinger's.

7. Pope John Paul II's General Audiences on Papal Infallibility

With regard to the principal argument of Part Two, it was brought to my attention that the thesis of the infallibility of the ordinary papal magisterium was contradicted by Pope John Paul II in a series of Wednesday Audiences which he gave on the subject of infallibility. In one audience he identifies 'ex cathedra' definitions with the 'solemn' exercise of the magisterium,[70] and then a week later, asserts that the pope speaks infallibly only when he speaks 'ex cathedra'.[71] Taking the two statements together, he thus appears to exclude the infallibility of the ordinary papal magisterium altogether. Such audiences are, of course, generally understood to be quite low on the scale of magisterial authority (they are not even published in the *Acta Apostolicae Sedis*), but out of respect for the pope I have eliminated references to the opposing position as a form of semi-Gallicanism. And although the arguments of Salaverri, Dublanchy, et al., still appear to me to be in themselves at least probable, I would no longer advance them as absolutely conclusive in the face of John Paul II's teaching.

However, it should also be noted that these Wednesday Audiences do nothing to resolve the problem posed by *Ordinatio*

---

[70] Pope John Paul II, *General Audience* (17 Mar. 1993): "Come è noto, ci sono dei casi nei quali il magistero pontificale si esercita solennemente su particolari punti di dottrina, appartenenti al deposito della rivelazione o ad essa strettamente connessi. È il caso delle *definizioni* 'ex cathedra', come quelle della Immacolata Concezione di Maria, fatta da Pio IX nel 1854, e della sua Assunzione al cielo, fatta da Pio XII nel 1950."

[71] Pope John Paul II, *General Audience* (24 Mar. 1993): "Infine, egli non la possiede come se potesse disporne o contarvi in ogni circostanza, ma solo 'quando parla dalla cattedra', e solo in un campo dottrinale limitato alle verità di fede e di morale e a quelle che vi sono strettamente connesse."

sacerdotalis with regard to its infallibility. A serious dilemma (or trilemma) remains. On the one hand, the central declaration of this Apostolic Letter appears to fulfill precisely the criteria for infallibility laid down by Vatican I, especially when the Vatican definition is read in light of Bishop Gasser's official explanation of the meaning of the word 'defines'. On the other hand, however, there is in the first place a common (although not unanimous) theological tradition, dating at least as far back as John Henry Newman, and now endorsed by Pope John Paul II in General Audience, which identifies papal infallibility exclusively with the extraordinary papal magisterium. And then there is also the fact that the CDF's *Doctrinal Commentary* on the Profession of Faith implies, and Ratzinger and Bertone state explicitly in separate articles in *L'Osservatore Romano*, that the declaration found in *Ordinatio sacerdotalis* is an exercise of the ordinary papal magisterium rather than of the extraordinary.

Now, any two of these points could be true, but not all three of them. It is not possible for *Ordinatio sacerdotalis* to be an infallible definition, and for it to be ordinary papal teaching, and for papal infallibility to be restricted to extraordinary teaching. The most commonly attempted resolution lies in the rejection of the first point, but I would question whether this is really the most reasonable approach. From the point of view of authority, one must compare (1) the authority of a general papal audience, (2) the opinions of an archbishop and a prominent cardinal expressed in a Roman newspaper, and (3) the official explanation of the spokesman of the deputation which drafted the text of the Vatican I definition. The highest degree of authority belongs to the Vatican definition itself, and it is not clear to me why Bishop Gasser's official explanation of this supremely authoritative text would be the least authoritative of the three texts in question.

Similarly, if one were to put aside questions of authority, the arguments of Salaverri and Dublanchy in favor of ordinary papal infallibility appear stronger than the bare assertion of Pope John Paul II against it. Nor do I find Ratzinger's argument in favor of the ordinariness of *Ordinatio sacerdotalis* very compelling since he premises his conclusion on the fact that the inability of the Church to ordain women to the priesthood had already been infallibly taught by the Church. The implied major premise of this argument could only be that it is not possible for the same doctrine to be solemnly defined more than once. This, however, would still need to be proven; and on the contrary, Pope Leo XIII seems to indicate that it is possible. Reiterating the Church's constant teaching on the material inerrancy of Scripture, he concludes by reminding his flock that, "This is the ancient and unchanging faith of the Church, solemnly defined in the Councils of Florence and of Trent."[72]

Why, then, should one conclude that *Ordinatio sacerdotalis* is not infallible because it is ordinary, rather than concluding that it is extraordinary because infallible, or indeed, that it is both ordinary and infallible? At the very least, I would submit that it is insufficient to reject the infallibility of *Ordinatio sacerdotalis* by appeal to the combined authority of Pope John Paul II in Wednesday Audience and Cardinal Ratzinger in *L'Osservatore Romano*, without also providing a plausible explanation as to where and how the declaration of *Ordinatio sacerdotalis* fails to meet Vatican I's criteria for infallibility as explained by Bishop Gasser.

---

[72] Pope Leo XIII, Encyclical Letter on the Study of Holy Scripture *Providentissimus Deus* (18 Nov. 1893), § 20: "Etenim libri omnes atque integri, quos Ecclesia tamquam sacros et canonicos recipit, cum omnibus suis partibus, Spiritu Sancto dictante, conscripti sunt; tantum vero abest ut divinae inspiratione error ullus subesse possit, ut ea per se ipsa, non modo errorem excludat omnem, sed tam necessario excludat et respuat, quam necessarium est, Deum, summam Veritatem, nullius omnino erroris auctorem esse. – Haec est antiqua et constans fides Ecclesiae, solemni etiam sententia in Conciliis definita Florentino et Tridentino. . ." (ASS 26 [1893–94]: 288).

BIBLIOGRAPHY OF WORKS CONSULTED

Documents of the Magisterium

Code of Canon Law (1917).

Code of Canon Law (1983).

Code of Canons of the Eastern Churches (1990).

Catéchisme de l'Eglise catholique (1992).

Catechism of the Catholic Church (1997).

Council of Chalcedon. Definition of Faith *Sancta et magna*. Session V. 22 October 451.

Council of Constantinople III. Exposition of Faith *Unigenitus Dei*. Session XVIII. 16 September 681.

Council of Vatican I. Dogmatic Constitution on the Catholic Faith *Dei Filius*. Session III. 24 April 1870.

_____. First Dogmatic Constitution on the Church of Christ *Pastor Aeternus*. Session IV. 18 July 1870.

Council of Vatican II. Dogmatic Constitution on the Church *Lumen gentium*. Session V. 21 November 1964.

_____. Dogmatic Constitution on Divine Revelation *Dei Verbum*. Session VIII. 18 November 1865.

Pope St Hormisdas. Epistle to the Bishops of Spain *Inter ea quae*. 2 April 517.

Pope St Leo I. Letter to Flavian of Constantinople *Lectis dilectionis*. 13 June 449.

Pope St Agatho. Letter to Constantine IV *Omnium bonorum spes*. 680.

Pope St Gregory VII. *Dictatus papae*. 1075.

Pope Boniface VIII. Bull *Unam sanctam*. 18 November 1302.

Pope Benedict XII. Bull *Benedictus Deus*. 29 January 1336.

Pope Nicholas V. Bull *Romanus Pontifex*. 8 January 1454.

Pope Sixtus IV. Bull *Licet ea*. 9 August 1479.

Pope Leo X. Bull *Exsurge Domine*. 15 June 1520.

Pope Pius IV. Bull *Iniunctum nobis*. 13 November 1565.

Pope Innocent X. Bull *Cum occasione*. 31 May 1653.

Pope Innocent XI. Bull *Caelestis Pastor*. 20 November 1687.

Pope Alexander VIII. Constitution *Inter multiplices*. 4 August 1690.

Pope Innocent XII. Brief *Cum alias*. 12 March 1699.

Pope Clement XI. Bull *Unigenitus*. 8 September 1713.

Pope Benedict XIV. Encyclical Letter on Usury and Other Dishonest Profit *Vix pervenit*. 1 November 1745.

Pope Pius VI. Bull *Auctorem fidei*. 28 August 1794.

Pope Gregory XVI. Encyclical Letter on Church and State to the Clergy of Switzerland *Commissum divinitus*. 17 May 1835.

Pope Pius IX. Encyclical Letter on Faith and Religion *Qui Pluribus*. 9 November 1846.

_____. Bull *Ineffabilis Deus*. 8 December 1854.

_____. Apostolic Letter to the Archbishop of Munich *Tuas libenter*. 21 December 1863.

_____. Encyclical Letter Condemning Current Errors *Quanta cura*. 8 December 1864.

Pope Leo XIII. Encyclical Letter on the Evils of Society *Inscrutabili Dei consilio*. 21 April 1878.

_____. Encyclical Letter on the Christian Constitution of States *Immortale Dei*. 1 November 1885.

_____. Encyclical Letter on Christians as Citizens *Sapientiae christianae*. 10 January 1890.

_____. Encyclical Letter on the Unity of the Church *Satis cognitum*. 29 June 1896.

_____. Bull *Apostolicae curae*. 15 September 1896.

_____. Encyclical Letter to the Archbishop of Baltimore *Testem benevolentiae*. 22 January 1899.

_____. Encyclical Letter on Consecration to the Sacred Heart *Annum sacrum*. 25 May 1899.

Pope St Pius X. Apostolic Letter *Notre Charge Apostolique*. 15 August 1910.

_____. Apostolic Letter Motu Proprio *Sacrorum antistitum*. 1 September 1910.

Pope Pius XI. Encyclical Letter on Religious Unity *Mortalium animos*. 6 January 1928.

_____. Encyclical Letter on Reparation to the Sacred Heart *Miserentissimus Redemptor*. 8 May 1928.

_____. Encyclical Letter on Christian Education *Divini illius Magistri*. 31 December 1929.

_____. Encyclical Letter on Christian Marriage *Casti connubii*. 31 December 1930.

Pope Pius XII. Encyclical Letter concerning Some False Opinions Threatening to Undermine the Foundations of Catholic Doctrine *Humani generis*. 12 August 1950.

_____. Apostolic Constitution *Munificentissimus Deus*. 1 November 1950.

_____. Encyclical Letter on the Supranationality of the Church *Ad sinarum gentem*. 7 October 1954.

_____. Encyclical Letter on Devotion to the Sacred Heart *Haurietis aquas*. 15 May 1956.

_____. Encyclical Letter on Communism and the Church in China *Ad apostolorum principis*. 29 June 1958.

Pope John XXIII. Encyclical Letter on the See of Peter as the Center of Christian Unity *Aeterna Dei sapientia*. 11 November 1961.

Pope Paul VI. Encyclical Letter on the Regulation of Birth *Humanae vitae*. 25 July 1968.

Pope John Paul II. *General Audience*. 10 March 1993.

_____. *General Audience*. 17 March 1993.

_____. *General Audience*. 24 March 1993.

_____. Apostolic Letter on Reserving Priestly Ordination to Men Alone *Ordinatio sacerdotalis*. 22 May 1994.

_____. Encyclical Letter on the Value and Inviolability of Human Life *Evangelium vitae*. 25 March 1995.

_____. *Address to Congregation for the Doctrine of the Faith*. 24 November 1995.

_____. Apostolic Letter Motu Proprio *Ad tuendam fidem*. 18 May 1998.

Congregation for the Doctrine of the Faith. *Formula deinceps adhibenda in casibus in quibus iure praescribitur Professio Fidei loco formulae Tridentinae et iuramenti antimodernistici*. 17 July 1967.

_____. Declaration in Defense of the Catholic Doctrine on the Church Against Certain Errors of the Present Day *Mysterium Ecclesiae*. 24 June 1973.

_____. *Letter to Father Charles Curran*. 25 July 1986.

_____. *Professio fidei et Iusiurandum fidelitatis in suscipiendo officio nomine Ecclesiae exercendo*. 1 July 1988.

_____. Instruction on the Ecclesial Vocation of the Theologian *Donum veritatis*. 24 May 1990.

_____. Response to a Proposed Dubium concerning the Teaching Contained in *Ordinatio sacerdotalis*. 28 October 1995.

_____. *Professio fidei et Iusiurandum fidelitatis in suscipiendo officio nomine Ecclesiae exercendo una cum nota doctrinali adnexa*. 29 June 1998.

Secondary Sources

Antón, Angel. *"Ordinatio sacerdotalis*: Algunas reflexiones de 'gnoseología teológica'." *Gregorianum* 75 (1994): 723–42.

Bainvel, Jean V. *De magisterio vivo et traditione*. Paris: Beauchesne, 1905.

Ballerini, Pietro. *De potestate ecclesiastica*. Rome: Propaganda Fide, 1850.

_____. *De vi ac ratione primatus romanorum pontificum et de ipsorum infallibilitate in definiendis controversiis fidei*. Edited by Elbert W. Westhoff. Westphalia: Deiters, 1845.

Balthasar, Hans Urs von. *The Office of Peter and the Structure of the Church*. Translated by Andrée Emery. San Francisco: Ignatius Press, 1986.

Bellamy, Julien M. *La théologie catholique au XIXe siècle*, Second Edition. Paris: Beauchesne, 1904.

Bellarmine, St Robert. *De controversiis christianae fidei adversus hujus temporis haereticos*. In *Opera omnia*, Volume 1. Edited by Xisto Riario Sforza. Naples: Giuliano, 1856.

Bertone, Tarcisio. "Magisterial Documents and Public Dissent." *L'Osservatore Romano* (29 January 1997): 6–7.

Betti, Umberto. "Considerazioni dottrinali." *Notitia* 25 (1989): 321–25.

Beumer, Johannes. "Sind päpstliche Enzykliken unfehlbar?" *Theologie und Glaube* 42 (1952): 262–69.

Billot, Louis. *Tractatus de Ecclesia Christi, sive continuatio theologiae de Verbo Incarnato*. Third Edition. Volume 1. Prati: Giachetti, 1909.

Boyle, John P. "The Ordinary Magisterium: Towards a History of the Concept." *Heythrop Journal* 20 (1979): 380–98; 21 (1980): 14–29.

Brinkmann, Bernhard. "Gibt es unfehlbare Äußerungen des 'Magisterium Ordinarium' des Papstes?" *Scholastik* 28 (1953): 202–21.

Butler, Cuthbert. *The Vatican Council: The Story Told from Inside in Bishop Ullathorne's Letters*. London: Longmans, Green and Co., 1930.

Butler, Scott, et al. *Jesus, Peter and the Keys: A Scriptural Handbook on the Papacy*. Santa Barbara, Cal.: Queenship, 1996.

Cappello, Felix. *De matrimonio*. Volume 5 of *Tractatus canonico-moralis de sacramentis iuxta Codicem juris canonici*. Seventh Edition. Turin; Rome: Marietti, 1961.

Cartechini, Sixtus. *De valore notarum theologicarum et de criteriis ad eas dignoscendas*. Rome: Gregorian University Press, 1951.

Caudron, Marc. "Magistère ordinaire et infaillibilité pontificale d'après la constitution 'Dei Filius'." *Ephemerides Theologicae Lovanienses* 36 (1960): 393–431.

Chirico, Peter L. "Infallibility: A Reply." *The Thomist* 44 (1980): 128–35.

_____. "Infallibility: Rapprochement between Küng and the Official Church?" *Theological Studies* 42 (1981): 529–60.

Choupin, Lucien. *Valeur des décisions doctrinales et disciplinaires du Saint-Siège*. Second Edition. Paris: Beauchesne, 1913.

Ciappi, Luigi. "Crisis of the Magisterium, Crisis of Faith." *The Thomist* 32 (1968): 147–70.

Congar, Yves. "Saint Thomas Aquinas and the Infallibility of the Papal Magisterium." *The Thomist* 38 (1974): 81–105.

Connery, John R. "The Non-Infallible Moral Teaching of the Church." *The Thomist* 51 (1987): 1–16.

Costanzo, Joseph F. *The Historical Credibility of Hans Kung: An Inquiry and Commentary*. North Quincy, Mass.: Christopher, 1979.

Costigan, Richard F. *The Consensus of the Church and Papal Infallibility: A Study in the Background of Vatican I*. Washington D.C.: Catholic University of America Press, 2005.

Curran, Charles E. *Faithful Dissent*. Kansas City: Sheed and Ward, 1986.

_____. *Loyal Dissent: Memoirs of a Catholic Theologian*. Washington, D.C.: Georgetown University Press, 2006.

_____, Editor. *Contraception: Authority and Dissent*. New York: Herder and Herder, 1969.

_____, et al. "Statement by Theologians." *New York Times* (31 July 1968).

_____, et al. *Dissent In and For the Church*. New York: Sheed and Ward, 1969.

_____, et al. *The Responsibility of Dissent: The Church and Academic Freedom*. New York: Sheed and Ward, 1969.

D'Ormesson, Wladimir. *The Papacy*. Translated by Michael Derrick. Volume 81 of *Twentieth Century Encyclopedia of Catholicism*. Edited by Henri Daniel-Rops. New York: Hawthorn Books, 1959.

De Guibert, Joseph. *De Christi Ecclesia*. Second Edition. Rome: Gregorian University Press, 1928.

DiNoia, J. A. "Communion and Magisterium: Teaching Authority and the Culture of Grace." *Modern Theology* 9 (1993): 403–18.

Dublanchy, Edmond. "Infaillibilité du Pape." In *Dictionnaire de théologie catholique*. Volume 7:1638–1717. Edited by Alfred Vacant and Eugène Mangenot. Paris: Libraire Letouzey et Ané, 1922.

Dulles, Avery. "Newman on Infallibility." *Theological Studies* 51 (1990): 434–49.

_____. *Magisterium: Teacher and Guardian of the Faith*. Ave Maria, Fl.: Sapientia Press, 2007.

Ernst, Harold E. "The Theological Notes and the Interpretation of Doctrine." *Theological Studies* 63 (2002): 813–25.

Fenton, Joseph C. "Infallibility in the Encyclicals." *American Ecclesiastical Review* 128 (1953): 177–98.

_____. "John Henry Newman and the Vatican Definition of Papal Infallibility." *American Ecclesiastical Review* 113 (1945): 300–320.

_____. "*Magisterium* and Jurisdiction in the Catholic Church." *American Ecclesiastical Review* 130 (1954): 194–201.

_____. "The Doctrinal Authority of Papal Allocutions." *American Ecclesiastical Review* 134 (1956): 109–17.

_____. "The Doctrinal Authority of Papal Encyclicals." *American Ecclesiastical Review* 121 (1949): 136–50, 210–20.

_____. "The *Humani generis* and the Holy Father's Ordinary Magisterium." *American Ecclesiastical Review* 125 (1951): 53–62.

_____. "The Local Church of Rome." *American Ecclesiastical Review* 122 (1950): 454–64.

_____. "The Necessity for the Definition of Papal Infallibility by the Vatican Council." *American Ecclesiastical Review* 115 (1946): 439–57.

_____. "The Papal Allocution *Si diligis*." *American Ecclesiastical Review* 131 (1954): 186–98.

_____. "The Question of Ecclesiastical Faith." *American Ecclesiastical Review* 128 (1953): 287–301.

_____. "The Religious Assent Due to the Teachings of Papal Encyclicals." *American Ecclesiastical Review* 123 (1950): 59–67.

_____. "The Requisites for an Infallible Pontifical Definition according to the Commission of Pope Pius IX." *American Ecclesiastical Review* 115 (1946): 376–84.

_____. "Two Solemn Pontifical Definitions." *American Ecclesiastical Review* 124 (1951): 52–61.

Fessler, Joseph. *The True and the False Infallibility of the Popes: A Controversial Reply to Dr. Schulte*. Third Edition. Translated by Ambrose St. John. London: Burns and Oates, 1875.

Figueiredo, Anthony J. *The Magisterium-Theology Relationship: Contemporary Theological Conceptions in the Light of Universal Church Teaching Since 1835 and the Pronouncements of the*

Bishops of the United States. Rome: Gregorian University Press, 2001.

Ford, John C., and Germain Grisez. "Contraception and the Infallibility of the Ordinary Magisterium." *Theological Studies* 39 (1978): 258–312.

Ford, John T. "Infallibility: A Review of Recent Studies." *Theological Studies* 40 (1979): 273–305.

_____. "Küng on Infallibility: A Review Article." *The Thomist* 35 (1971): 501–12.

Franzelin, Johann Baptist. *Tractatus de divina traditione et scriptura*. Rome: Propaganda Fide; Turin: Marietti, 1870.

Gaillardetz, Richard R. "The Ordinary Universal Magisterium: Unresolved Questions." *Theological Studies* 63 (2002): 447–471.

_____. *Teaching with Authority: A Theology of the Magisterium in the Church*. Collegeville, Minn.: Liturgical Press, 1997.

Galvin, John P. "Papal Primacy in Contemporary Roman Catholic Theology." *Theological Studies* 47 (1986): 653–67.

George, Francis. "God's Point of View: Apostolicity and the Magisterium. A Lecture Delivered to the St. Anselm Institute at the University of Virginia." *Nova et Vetera* 6 (2008): 271–90.

Granderath, Theodor. *Geschichte des vatikanischen Konzils: von seiner ersten Ankündigung bis zu seiner Vertagung*. Edited by Konrad Kirch. Freiburg: Herder, 1903–1906.

Gres-Gayer, Jacques M. "The Magisterium of the Faculty of Theology of Paris in the Seventeenth Century." *Theological Studies* 53 (1992): 424–50.

_____. "The *Unigenitus* of Clement XI: A Fresh Look at the Issues." *Theological Studies* 49 (1998): 259–282.

Grisez, Germain. "Infallibility and Contraception: A Reply to Garth Hallett." *Theological Studies* 47 (1986): 134–45.

_____. "Infallibility and Specific Moral Norms: A Review Discussion." *The Thomist* 46 (1985): 248–87.

_____. "Magisterium and Infallibility: Response to Francis Sullivan's Reply." *Theological Studies* 55 (1994): 737–38.

_____. "The Ordinary Magisterium's Infallibility: A Reply to Some New Arguments." *Theological Studies* 55 (1994): 720–32.

Gutwenger, Englebert. "The Role of the Magisterium." *Concilium* 1.6 (1970): 43–55.

Hallett, Garth L. "Contraception and Prescriptive Infallibility." *Theological Studies* 43 (1982): 629–50.

_____. "Infallibility and Contraception: The Debate Continues." *Theological Studies* 49 (1988): 517–28.

Harrison, Brian W. "The *Ex Cathedra* Status of the Encyclical *Humanae Vitae*." *Living Tradition* 43 (Sep.–Nov. 1992).

Hennessy, Paul K. "Episcopal Collegiality and Papal Primacy in the Pre-Vatican I American Church." *Theological Studies* 44 (1983): 288–97.

_____. "Infallibility in the Ecclesiology of Peter Richard Kenrick." *Theological Studies* 45 (1984): 702–14.

Hettinger, Franz. *Supremacy of the Apostolic See in the Church.* Translated by George Porter. London: Burns and Oates; New York: Catholic Publication Society, 1889.

Horst, Ulrich. *Papst-Konzil-Unfehlbarkeit: Die Ekklesiologie der Summen-kommentare von Cajetan bis Billuart*. Mainz: Matthias-Grünewald, 1978.

_____. *Unfehlbarkeit und Geschichte: Studien zur Unfehlbarkeitsdiskussion von Melchior Cano bis zum I. Vatikanischen Konzil*. Mainz: Matthias-Grünewald, 1982.

Hughes, Gerald J. "Infallibility in Morals." *Theological Studies* 34 (1973): 415–28.

Hughes, John J. "Hans Küng and the Magisterium." *Theological Studies* 41 (1980): 368–89.

_____. "Infallible? An Inquiry Considered." *Theological Studies* 32 (1971): 183–207.

Hünermann, Peter, and Dietmar Mieth, Editors. *Streitgespräch um Theologie und Lehramt: Die Instruktion über die kirchliche Berufung des Theologen in der Diskussion*. Frankfurt: Knecht, 1991.

Hünermann, Peter. "Schwerwiegende Bedenken: Eine Analyse des Apostolischen Schreibens 'Ordinatio Sacerdotalis'." *Herder Korrespondenz* 48 (1994): 406–10.

Hurley, Denis E. "Population Control and the Catholic Conscience: Responsibility of the Magisterium." *Theological Studies* 35 (1974): 154–63.

Journet, Charles. *The Primacy of Peter: From the Protestant and from the Catholic Point of View*. Translated by John Chapin. Westminster: Newman Press, 1954.

Kenrick, Francis. *Theologiae dogmaticae tractatus tres: de revelatione, de Ecclesia, et de Verbo Dei*. Philadelphia: Johnson, 1839.

Kleutgen, Joseph. *Die Theologie der Vorzeit verteidigt.* Second Edition. Volume 1. Innsbruck: Rauch, 1878.

Küng, Hans. *Unfehlbar? Eine Anfrage.* Zürich: Benzinger, 1970.

Kwasniewski, Peter A. "The Authority of Papal Encyclicals." *Lay Witness* (March/April 2007): 54–55.

Lamont, John R. T. "Determining the Content and Degree of Authority of Church Teachings." *The Thomist* 72 (2008): 371–407.

Landgraf, A. M. "Scattered Remarks on the Development of Dogma and on Papal Infallibility in Early Scholastic Writings." *Theological Studies* 7 (1946): 577–82.

Levillain, Phillipe, and John W. O'Malley, Editors. *The Papacy: An Encyclopedia.* New York: Routledge, 2002.

Lio, Ermenegildo. *Humanae Vitae e Infallibilità: il Concilio, Paolo VI e Giovanni Paolo II.* Vatican City: Libreria Editrice Vaticana, 1986.

Lutheran-Roman Catholic Dialogue. "Teaching Authority and Infallibility in the Church." *Theological Studies* 40 (1979): 113–66.

Manning, Henry Edward. *The Centenary of St. Peter and the General Council: A Pastoral Letter to the Clergy.* London: Longmans, Green, and Co., 1867.

_____. *The Oecumenical Council and the Infallibility of the Roman Pontiff: A Pastoral Letter to the Clergy.* Second Edition. London: Longmans, Green, and Co., 1869.

_____. *The True Story of the Vatican Council.* London: Henry King, 1877.

_____. *The Vatican Council and Its Definitions: A Pastoral Letter to the Clergy.* London: Longmans, Green, and Co., 1870.

_____. *The Vatican Decrees in Their Bearing on Civil Allegiance.* London: Longmans, Green, and Co., 1875.

May, William E. "The Cultural and Ecclesial Situation 1964 to 1967: Paving the Way for Dissent From Church Teaching on Contraception." *Nova et Vetera* 7 (2009): 711–29.

May, William W., Editor. *Vatican Authority and American Catholic Dissent: The Curran Case and Its Consequences.* New York: Crossroad, 1987.

Melina, Livio. "The Role of the Ordinary Magisterium: On Francis Sullivan's *Creative Fidelity.*" *The Thomist* 61 (1997): 605–15.

Merry del Val, Raphael. *The Truth of Papal Claims.* London: Sands; St. Louis: Herder, 1904.

Morris, Eugene S. "The Infallibility of the Apostolic See in Jaun de Torquemada O.P." *The Thomist* 46 (1982): 242–66.

Müller, Gerhard L. *Katholische Dogmatik: Für Studium und Praxis der Theologie.* Freiburg: Herder, 2005.

Nau, Paul. "The Ordinary Magisterium of the Catholic Church." In *Pope or Church? Essays on the Infallibility of the Ordinary Magisterium.* Translated by Arthur E. Slater. Kansas City: Angelus Press, 2006.

Naud, André. *Devant la nouvelle profession de foi et le serment de fidélité.* Montreal: Fides, 1989.

_____. *Le magistère incertain.* Montreal: Fides, 1987.

Newman, John Henry. *A Letter Addressed to His Grace the Duke of Norfolk on Occasion of Mr. Gladstone's Recent Expostulation.* London: Pickering, 1875.

O'Connor, James T, Translator. *The Gift of Infallibility: The Official Relatio on Infallibility of Bishop Vincent Gasser at Vatican Council I.* Boston: St. Paul Editions, 1986.

O'Meara, Thomas F. "Divine Grace and Human Nature as Sources for the Universal Magisterium of Bishops." *Theological Studies* 64 (2003): 683–706.

Oeing-Hanhoff, Ludger. "Ist das kirchliche Lehramt für den Bereich des Sittlichen zuständig?" *Theologische Quartalschrift* 161 (1981): 56–66.

Orsi, Giuseppe-Agostino. *De irreformabili romani pontifici in definiendis fidei controversiis judicio.* Rome: Junchius, 1771.

Orsy, Ladislas. "Magisterium: Assent and Dissent." *Theological Studies* 48 (1987): 473–97.

_____. *Receiving the Council: Theological and Canonical Insights and Debates.* Collegeville, Minn.: Liturgical Press, Michael Glazier, 2009.

Ott, Ludwig. *Fundamentals of Catholic Dogma.* Edited by James Bastible. Translated by Patrick Lynch. Rockford, Ill.: Tan Books, 1974.

Palmieri, Dominico. *Tractatus de romano pontifice cum prolegomeno de Ecclesia.* Prati, 1891.

Perrone, Giovanni. *De romani pontificis infallibilitate, seu Vaticana definitio contra novos hereticos asserta et vindicata.* Turin: Marietti, 1874.

_____. *Praelectiones theologicae*. Twenty-Sixth Edition. Paris: Leroux, Jouby, et Cie, 1854.

Pesch, Christian. *Compendium theologiae dogmaticae*. Volume 1. Fribourg: Herder, 1913.

Pink, Thomas. "What Is the Catholic Doctrine of Religious Liberty?" Paper read at the Februrary 2010 Aquinas Seminar, Blackfriars, Oxford.

Pottmeyer, Hermann J. *Towards a Papacy in Communion: Perspectives from Vatican Councils I and II*. Translated by Matthew J. O'Connell. New York: Crossroad, Herder and Herder, 1998.

Powell, Mark E. *Papal Infallibility: A Protestant Evaluation of an Ecumenical Issue*. Grand Rapids: Eerdmans, 2009.

Prendergast, R. S. "Some Neglected Factors of the Birth Control Question." *Sciences Ecclesiastiques* 18 (1966): 218–19.

Quinn, John R. *The Reform of the Papacy: The Costly Call to Christian Unity*. New York: Crossroad, Herder and Herder, 1999.

Rahner, Karl. "Dogmatic Constitution on the Church, Chapter III, Articles 18–27." Translated by Kevin Smyth. In Volume 1 of *Commentary on the Documents of Vatican II*. Edited by Herbert Vorgrimler. London: Burns and Oates; New York: Herder and Herder, 1967.

Ratzinger, Joseph. "The Limits of Church Authority." *L'Osservatore Romano* (29 June 1994): 6–8.

_____. *Jesus of Nazareth*, Volume 1. Translated by Adrian J. Walker. New York: Doubleday, 2007. Volume 2. Translated by Philip J. Whitmore. San Francisco: Ignatius Press, 2011.

_____. "Letter Concerning the CDF Reply Regarding *Ordinatio Sacerdotalis.*" *L'Osservatore Romano* (19 November 1995).

_____. *The Nature and Mission of Theology: Approaches to Understanding Its Role in the Light of Present Controversy.* Translated by Adrian Walker. San Francisco: Ignatius Press, 1995.

Sala, Giovanni. "Fallible Teachings and the Assistance of the Holy Spirit: Reflections on the Ordinary Magisterium in Connection with the Instruction on the Ecclesial Vocation of the Theologian." *Nova et Vetera* 4 (2006): 29–54.

Salaverri, Joachim. "Valor de las encíclicas a la luz de la 'Humani generis'." *Miscelánea Comillas* 10.17 (1952): 134–71.

_____. *Tractatus de Ecclesia Christi.* In *Theologia fundamentalis,* Volume 1 of *Sacrae theologiae summa.* Fifth Edition. Madrid: Biblioteca de Autores Cristianos, 1962.

Santogrossi, Ansgar. "*Ordinatio Sacerdotalis*: A Definition *ex cathedra.*" *Homiletic and Pastoral Review* (Feb. 1999): 7–14.

Schatz, Klaus. *Der Päpstliche Primat: seine Geschichte von den Ursprüngen bis zur Gegenwart.* Würzburg: Echter, 1990.

_____. "Welche bisherigen päpstlichen Lehrentscheidungen sind 'ex cathedra'? Historische und theologische Überlegungen." In *Dogmengeschichte und katholische Theologie,* 404–22. Edited by Werner Löser, Karl Lehmann, and Matthias Lutz-Bachmann. Würzburg: Echter, 1985.

Scheeben, Matthias J. *Theologische Erkenntnislehre.* Volume 1 of *Handbuch der Katholischen Dogmatik.* Third Edition. Edited by Martin Grabmann. Freiburg: Herder, 1959.

Schmaus, Michael. *Katholische Dogmatik*. Sixth Edition. Volume 1. Munich: Hueber, 1960.

_____. *The Church: Its Origin and Structure*. Volume 4 of *Dogma*. London: Sheed and Ward, 1972.

Schmied, Augustin. "'Schleichende Infallibilisierung': Zur Diskussion um das kirchliche Lehramt." In *In Christus zum Leben befreit: Festschrift für Bernhard Häring*, 250–72. Edited by Josef Römelt and Bruno Hidber. Freiburg; Basel; Vienna: Herder, 1992.

Sesboüé, Bernard. "Magistère 'ordinaire' et magistère authentique." *Recherches de science religieuse* 84 (1996): 267–75.

Sheehan, Michael. *Apologetics*, Sixth Edition and *Catholic Doctrine*, Fourth Edition. Revised and Edited by Peter M. Joseph. London: Saint Austin Press, 2001.

Spohn, William C. "The Magisterium and Morality." *Theological Studies* 54 (1993): 95–111.

Stirnimann, Heinrich. "'Magisterio enim ordinario haec docentur.' Zur einer Kontroversstelle der Enzyklika 'Humani generis'," *Freiburger Zeitschrift für Philosophie und Theologie* 1 (1954): 17–47.

Sullivan, Francis A. "Infallible Teaching on Moral Issues? Reflections on Veritatis Splendor and Evangelium Vitae." In *Choosing Life: A Dialogue on* Evangelium Vitae. Edited by Kevin W. Wildes and Alan C. Mitchell. Washington, D.C.: Georgetown University Press, 2007.

_____. "New Claims for the Pope." *The Tablet* 248 (18 June 1994): 767–69.

_____. "Recent Theological Observations on Magisterial Documents and Public Dissent." *Theological Studies* 58 (1997): 509–15.

_____. "Reply to Lawrence J. Welsh." *Theological Studies* 64 (2003): 610–15.

_____. "Some Observations on the New Formula for the Profession of Faith." *Gregorianum* 70 (1989): 549–58.

_____. "The Meaning of Conciliar Dogmas." In *The Convergence of Theology: A Festschrift Honoring Gerald O'Collins, S.J.*, 73–86. Edited by Daniel Kendall and Stephen T. Davis. Mahwah, N.J.: Paulist Press, 2001.

_____. "The 'Secondary Object' of Infallibility." *Theological Studies* 54 (1993): 536–50.

_____. "The Doctrinal Weight of *Evangelium Vitae*." *Theological Studies* 56 (1995): 560–65.

_____. "The Ordinary Magisterium's Infallibility: A Reply to Germain Grisez." *Theological Studies* 55 (1994): 732–37.

_____. "The Teaching Authority of Episcopal Conferences." *Theological Studies* 63 (2002): 472–93.

_____. "The Theologian's Ecclesial Vocation and the 1990 CDF Instruction." *Theological Studies* 52 (1991): 51–68.

_____. *Creative Fidelity*. New York; Mahwah, N.J.: Paulist Press, 1996.

_____. *Magisterium: Teaching Authority in the Catholic Church*. New York; Mahwah, N.J.: Paulist Press, 1983.

_____. *Quaestiones theologiae fundamentalis.* Volume 1 of *De Ecclesia.* Rome: Gregorian University Press, 1963.

_____. *Salvation Outside the Church? Tracing the History of the Catholic Response.* Eugene, Ore.: Wipf and Stock, 2002.

Tanquerey, Adolphe. *Sysnopsis theologiae dogmaticae fundamentalis.* Twenty-Fourth Edition. Paris: Desclée, 1937.

Ter Haar, Francis. *De praecipuis hujus aetatis vitiis eorumque remediis.* Volume 2 of *Casus conscientiae.* Turin; Rome: Marietti, 1939.

Thils, Gustave. *L'infaillibilité pontifical: Source, conditions, limites.* Gembloux: Duculot, 1969.

Tierney, Brian. "Infallibility in Morals: A Response." *Theological Studies* 35 (1974): 507–17.

_____. "John Peter Olivi and Papal Inerrancy: On a Recent Interpretation of Olivi's Ecclesiology." *Theological Studies* 46 (1985): 315–28.

_____. *Origins of Papal Infallibility, 1150–1350: A Study on the Concepts of Infallibility, Sovereignty and Tradition in the Middle Ages.* Leiden: Brill, 1972.

Ullathorne, William. *Mr. Gladstone's Expostulation Unravelled.* New York: Catholic Publication Society, 1875.

Vacant, J.-M. Alfred. *Le magistère ordinaire de l'Eglise et ses organes.* Paris; Lyons: Delhomme et Briguet, 1887.

Welch, Lawrence J. "Reply to Richard Gaillardetz on the Ordinary Universal Magisterium and to Francis Sullivan." *Theological Studies* 64 (2003): 598–609.

_____. "The Infallibility of the Ordinary Universal Magisterium: A Critique of Some Recent Observations." *Heythrop Journal* 39 (1998): 18–36.

Wilson, George B. "The Gift of Infallibility: Reflections Toward a Systematic Theology." *Theological Studies* 31 (1970): 625–43.

NOTES